T0365207

Life...
Yesterday, Today,
and Tomorrow

Also by Jeanette Dowdell

Something For Everyone With Love (poetry)
Heavenly Mysteries (children's book)
The Hereafter
Our Next Assignment, Our Next Grand Adventure
(Religion – Multi-media)

Life...
Yesterday, Today, and Tomorrow

A Potpourri of Poetry

JEANETTE DOWDELL

LIFE... YESTERDAY, TODAY, AND TOMORROW
A POTPOURRI OF POETRY

iUniverse books may be ordered through booksellers or by contacting:

iUniverse
1663 Liberty Drive
Bloomington, IN 47403
www.iuniverse.com
1-800-Authors (1-800-288-4677)

ISBN: 978-1-5320-3930-0 (sc)
ISBN: 978-1-5320-3929-4 (e)

Library of Congress Control Number: 2018900802

Print information available on the last page.

iUniverse rev. date: 07/30/2018

Dedication

I lovingly dedicate this work to those who knew me best

Mabel G. Dowdell, Mother
John R. Dowdell, Brother

Life

Life is like a million or more bubbles
floating in all directions
searching perhaps for
the " real" in reality

Preface

It is not only a pleasure, but a privilege to be able to share my thoughts with you. I hope that they will not only be interesting, but inspiring in some way. Perhaps you will find that we walked the same paths, were taught and learned the same ways of life. Is it possible you and I feel deeply about the same things? Or, view life, faith, family, friends, nature, love, pets, and share them with the same intensity? That could be. And, wouldn't that be a miracle? Life is a miracle filled with magic.

Since you are taking the time to read my words, I hope you find them to be filled with magic also. I hope you find something special as you read, something to share, perhaps a poem or two to commit to memory, one that will follow you forever, one to share with others in the future – tomorrow. If that happens, happy I will be. Enjoy!

Life – Yesterday, Today and Tomorrow

Acknowledgement

Judy K. Meserve
Patient
Kind
Patient
Caring
Patient
Warm
Patient
Happy
Patient
Unperturbable
(And don't think I didn't try)
Patient
Patient – Patient

Words fail me.
There are no words equal to the time given,
the sharing of thoughts and knowledge,
joy and laughter, and the most
appreciated thoughtful critiques.
This was friendship beyond what I deserved and value.
A life's blessing.

Thank you, my friend.

A special thanks also to my friends, Flo,
Gladys and Marilyn for their kindness,
thoughtfulness, encouragement and support

Contents

TODAY

TOMORROW

Yesterday

Yesterday is an imposter. Not too long ago it was known as today. It actually looked forward to becoming tomorrow. And, if we live long enough, today will become yesterday and tomorrow. So, I have decided to begin my poetic journey with a potpourri of poetry in my world of yesterday.

I will share with you my favorite moments. You know those from times gone by. Many yesterdays…those that the following memoir-like poems attest to…memories shelved, yet very much alive. Let it be known however that I do not live in the world of yesterday, I simply visit.

Where shall I begin? Family? Friends? My life's beginning?

Associates? How about with a myriad of precious thoughts?

I think I will start at a point after the demise of those I dedicated this book to – those who knew me best, my mother, totally unselfish, all giving, all loving and my brother, who I will simply define as being extremely talented, and always being what he wanted to be. Both obviously remembered. Then, I will address my life's beginning and move forward to some of yesterday's precious moments.

Years Gone By

Remembering:
Mabel G. Dowdell, Mother
August 6, 1974

It is many years since my mom drew her last breath,
Yet I remember that time as if it were today,
I remember how grateful and how heartbroken I was,
She moaned for days before God reached down to ease her pain,
Before He heard her, and my prayers,
Before He drew her last breath and gave her comfort and peace,
Before He moved her into her new home,

Remembering – that's what love is all about – *remembering,*

An everlasting memory includes the
aggregate of all the love lived in

Years Gone By

We Will Waltz Again

In Memoriam
J. R. Dowdell, brother
January 31, 2007

There comes a time when we all must part,
That's known from our very start,
But, when loved ones leave, they rarely leave the heart,
And memory upon memory, the mind continues to impart,
Since my brother was the last to travel yonder,
His memories still flood the mind and grow fonder,
The one that shines the brightest by far,
Is the dancing we did in our youth...star-to-star,
Gliding and floating in heaven to each refrain,
It is not forgotten or lost; someday

We Will Waltz Again

My Journeys

Out of the Universe my soul was delivered
by the Hand of God,
The journey was as swift as creation itself,
as startling as a lightning rod,
Because of its speed,
that journey was short, without a bump,
And there I was in a cocoon; a quiet, pulsating lump,
A foreigner nestled warm and snug,
within a womb somewhere,
Where? – Should I guess? – Do I dare?
Will I be human, or an animal in the forest deep?
Soon I will know, after I grow out of my present sleep,
I'm tired from my journey, and now I'm living in another,
Dealing with tight quarters and someone else's food –
trying not to smother,
I wonder how my mother-to-be feels, when I move,
When I'm out of sorts, give 'er a kick – lose my groove?
I don't know why I have this string attached to me,
Or how I will get out of here; what a ride that will be,
I cannot stay here forever,
Where is the 'exit' lever?
Pretty soon, I'll be able to tell
if I am a he or a she, I guess,
If not, my life's going to be an awful mess,
How come I can think; after all,
I am still journeying in growth mode,
What if I am born a spider or a toad?
No, I have passed that size; I am too big,

And listen to my vocabulary; 'pretty cool' – dig?
Gosh, I know I am living in a ball,
It sometimes crashes,
and at other times, stands tall,
And all the time I am supposed to be quiet –
barely known,
But that is impossible, for I have grown
and grown and grown,
Oh, by the way, I am a 'he,'
I have a spigot,
that every now and then, 'washes' me,
'Hey guys,' I am getting real cramped;
how do I get out of here?
It must be time for a new,
bright, clean atmosphere,
'Don't get so pushy, I am upside down,
Ease up; what are you, a clown?
I am losin' my grip,
I am beginnin' to slip,'
Oh, my, you are pushing
my head through that small hole,
Wow! It sure is bright –
Another journey? Another role?
Why am I upside down; is
someone holding me by my feet?
Will I have to walk like this on the street?
Ow! Stop doin' that or I will scream and cry,
Put me right side up, and let go of my foot,
so I can kick you in the eye,
What kind of new beginning is this?
Hey, my feeding tube is gone;
somethin's really amiss,
It couldn't get any brighter,
but it is nice and warm,
Let me just say,

'this has been quite a transforming storm,'
I am tired; I think I'll take a short rest,
My journey's just beginning and already
I have been put to the test,
What color am I anyway?
And, who are all those people gazing this way?
Every part of me is covered;
I cannot tell my color, or shade,
Funny thing, once I didn't hit 'the bucket,'
I knew I had it made,
Thank you, God, for protecting me,
I will be special, you wait and see,
You breathed Your breath of life
into my soul and wee frame,
My faith will be strong; never one to defame,
I promise, now and forever, I will be true,
And I can say that
even after what I have just been put through,
Oh, my, I am all wet, and wrapped in my what?
And, I can't help myself; 'Change me now,
or I will scream, and cause a riot,'
How long will I have to live like this, dirty and wet,
'Oh, who is this lovely person?
Seems to me, we have met,'
Oh, that is much better;
I am warm and dry, being lifted aloft,
I am being cradled, and sung too,
and pressed against something soft,
I think that I shall take a nap,
And I promise, I will not wail again,
until my diaper is full of ......
That is not nice, I will just say, 'duty,'
That is really a bit of beauty,
A bit of this, a bit of that,
And now I am at the end of the line,

How did I get here so fast – out of time?
Wherever did the time go?
Pretty soon, you will call me home, whoa,
Can't believe my time is up,
I still feel as frisky as a pup,
There is a reason why I made the beginning meet
the end so quickly; it is a simple demonstration of time,
It moves so fast – too fast, and that is a crime,
I do hope that I kept my promise
through my years – not to displease,
Thank You for a life filled with beautiful moments
and memories throughout …

My Journeys

Shoes

Shoes? Who needs shoes?

My mom loved to tell this story about me,
when I was just a "wee tot,"
Practically new born;
every day she would get me (perfect) 'spit-spot'
before she would present me to the neighbors,
I was about two to three months old,
just a baby in my carriage/, perambulator
An old fashioned high baby buggy,
"a coach carriage"
My mom, as she noted was beside herself, because
I would not keep my white high-top shoes on,
No matter what she did,
I would simply remove my shoes,
Without untying them I would somehow
slip them off, and throw them out of my buggy
She would find them on the ground,

She knew she had tied them tight,
but baby didn't care,
Each time she returned,
they would be on the ground, still tied,
I always wondered, but never asked,
"Did I giggle?"
I guess even then I was projecting my strongest
lifelong negative – stubbornness,
Ask anyone, I admit it,

Shoes? Who needs shoes?

To this day, as old as I am, on the downside of the hill,
I am still having trouble with shoes, tied or untied.

A Child Within

A spirit from the past,
The one you want to last,
Oh, wouldn't you like to run and fall,
as a child?
Eat and drink as before – go wild?
Play softball, baseball, tennis and stickball, too?
How about basketball,
volley ball, to name but a few,
I roller skated, and ice skated and climbed trees,
I challenged my fear, and dealt with scraped knees,
I loved track, and punch ball, diving and swimming, too,
And before I knew it, my childhood was gone; I grew,
And every day since,
I've regretted the loss of my childish ways,
I have always wanted to go back, relive those days,
"Doesn't anyone feel as I?" so I say with a grin,
Come on, admit it, we all still have...

A Child Within

Surprise

'A five sense tour de force'

Years ago when I was a 'wee-tot,'
I thought about 'surprise' a lot,
They would put surprises in cereal boxes
and Cracker Jacks,
There were gimmicks and give-backs,
Radio programs geared towards kids
would offer all sorts of things,
Coloring books, wrist bands,
and magic plastic rings,
Comic books were like 'daytime serials'
to be continued next week,
We would wait for a surprise to come;
given that mind tweak,
What fun we had at a much slower pace,
Our childhood did not run
through life yelling, 'erase, erase,'
We did not have what children have today,
But somehow we had time to enjoy it more;
less might be a better way,
For you remember flavors
and tastes that still linger on,
The creators of which are long gone,
The surprises of a texture and taste
that lasts as long as you do,

That is a surprise in itself;
however I would love a new review,
Surprises came packaged in all shapes
and sizes, to say the least,
Isn't it wonderful how the memory recalls
the memory of each little beast?
Does it only belong to the memory of the most wise?
No, only the one who recalls until death,
the endless joy of each life's...

Surprise

Desire

I wanted to run and swim the fastest,
Climb the highest,
bat the longest homerun, pitch the perfect game,
Have the highest basketball score,
Be in every inning of the Softball Game,
Pitch, play first, second and third base,
short-stop, left, center and right fields,
That wasn't asking too much, was it?
There was one position I never wanted to play,
That was catcher,
So you see,
there was always one position left for others,
And when I was not running around the track,
I wanted to play volley ball,
Stick ball, tennis, football, handball, and skate,
Winter or summer, it didn't matter,
I reached out to every sport,
Unsupervised most times,
When I skated,
I skated down "Deadman's Hill" on roller skates,
I would skate on any patch of ice,
Or in the Rockefeller Ice Skating Rink
when my uncle would take me,
And what I really enjoyed was skating
in the indoor Roller Rink,
It was warm,
And the music was great,
I learned to turn, roll backwards, twirl, and

lean back to sail along those shiny rink boards,
How thrilled was I
when I received my new white, high-top roller skates?
They were in a bright red carry case
Do not laugh, I still have them,
I grew out of my beautiful ice skates,
So, I gave them away, for someone else to enjoy,
Hey, I'm not through,
How about the parallel bars in the playground?
They held a great attraction,
I thought that I was an Olympic star,
I never gave a thought to the fact
that they were hovering over cement,
And when I asked for a baseball mitt for my birthday,
my mother would have no part in buying
"her little girl," a baseball mitt,
So I played without one
unless one of the "boys" would share,
Some did, but none on the other team,
One thing was for certain,
What I lacked in brains and talent, never mattered,
For I was filled with something the others lacked,
no matter what the sport,
I was filled with the greatest, innate, burning

Desire

The High Diving Board

I sat poolside, looking up at the high diving board,
I watched as others climbed the ladder;
sailed off, over, and into the water,
I wanted so to sail as they sailed,
I had never attempted a dive off a high board,
I was never trained,
But somehow I knew before I left that pool,
I would take that plunge,
And I would not jump; I would dive,
I stood at the base of the ladder for a long time,
and prayed,
My knees shook with fear, but I was determined,
It was a beautiful sunny and warm day
And the Day Liner would be waiting to take me home,
I climbed higher and higher,
I finally reached the top,
I walked forward with great confidence
to the end of the board,
And when I looked down, I almost died,
But I was still full of determination,
I adjusted my cap,
and headed head first towards the water,
Let's just say, "I lived to tell this story,"
My bathing cap split from end to end,
My head however, stayed in one piece,
That was my first and my last attempt to

sail off a high diving board,
Parents really never know,
what their children are doing,
To me, it was just another challenge,
just another experience,
Just another something to write about,
Death and injury never entered my mind,
Simply the eight-foot flight off

The High Diving Board

The Local Grocery Store

Step in the door; get a wonderfully warm, 'Hello!'
Everything was fresh and displayed just so,
The vegetables and fruits were washed and clean,
In summer, individual pieces of watermelon
were on ice placed to be seen,
Bread was 'squeeze-ably' fresh, and piled high,
Cereals and dry goods were stacked on shelves
reaching the sky,
And on the counter, candies and cookies
smiled in jars and bags,
Attracted kids of all ages –
some in tatters and rags,
Some were sold two pieces for a penny,
But without the penny, you learned to say,
'No thanks, I don't want any,'
And, if you behaved while in the store,
The owner would put a little treat in the bag…
a caramel or two, or three, or four,
Not every time; otherwise it wouldn't be a treat,
And what child would turn down a sweet?
Nothing was sanitized or wrapped as things are today,
And no one gave it a thought; that was the way,
No dates, limited refrigeration, no wrappings;
flies all over the place,
Funny thing, we survived and
everyone had a smile on their face,

In the hottest days of summer when the air was stale,
lights were dimmed, and fans would roar,
And who could ever forget
the slammin' screen door at ...

The Local Grocery Store

17

I Enjoyed Being Spoiled

Years ago, I would walk into
the local grocery store with a list,
I would wait my turn and read the items;
the clerk would get the gist,
He would know where each item was in his store,
And I was not permitted to explore,
Fruits, vegetables, dried and canned goods
were all in their place,
Only the clerk would handle the produce,
and rearrange each vacant space,
I can still picture them holding up a bunch of
grapes and removing those less than perfect,
They rarely gave their steady customers
any duds, or a reject,
They knew you would return it,
if anything was not just so,
And if they pulled a fast one,
they knew you would know,
They wanted their customers to be pleased,
Pass a negative comment,
and you would quickly be appeased,
Whatever they sold, whatever they said,
their reputation was on the line,
And even if you did not shop on a specific day,
they would check to see if everything was fine,
Nothing was dated;
they knew what was fresh, what was stale,
They would wink or say,

18

"Wait a day; it is going on sale,"
Meaning, 'steer clear' it is not
as fresh as you would like,
Another thing, you could only buy
what you could carry; we all had a hike,
And very often you would run out of money;
things were tight,
They would always give you credit
'til your next pay night,
There was trust and friendship,
and always a helping hand,
One store, no aisle upon aisle;
it was simple nothing "super-grand,"
You had less to spend then, never more,
Sometimes you would have to wait a week
for things to come into the store,
Selections were few, but you got used to that,
You did not miss what you did not see;
service was tops, lots of chit-chat,
I guess that was what a neighborhood store
was all about,
You felt safe; strangers stood out,
We had so much less; but actually more,
When we shopped in the local grocery store,
They plied their trade well, and they really toiled,
And I didn't know then,
but I do now; how very much

I Enjoyed Being Spoiled
**(Brown paper bags on which prices were listed,
added in the head – 'nough said!)**

Some Of The Things I Really Miss

Part 1
"My Vanity Showeth"

I miss using make-up, which I loved,
It was always a joy to match the color
of my clothes with my eye shadow,
Then coordinate those colors
with my nail polish,
I would stay awake into the wee-hours
to be so matched,
And that could go on every night,
It was never a chore, it was a delight,
And to think about matching a hat,
a coat, shoes and gloves,
Wow!
Well, there were times
when the perfect match could not be found,

But then, to be more creative,
I'd find the perfect color-blend,
What could be more thrilling?
Many things I suppose,
But that certainly was fun,
And when others recognized my efforts,
it was all worthwhile just to hear someone say,
"Oh, I love that combination of colors,"
That was well worth fewer sleep hours,
Now, some might call that vanity,
but certainly I did not,
It was more in the vain of wanting to say,
"I took the time to put myself together for you,"
Of course, this does date me,
You know, gloves, matching colors,
nail polish, and eye-shadow,
I failed to mention the shoes
were two- and three-inch spikes,
It was like walking on a three-inch hardware nail,
And when the style changed to "pointy-toed shoes,"
Who could resist?
Ankles and calves took on a sexier look,
They shrunk, by God,
And attracted many an eye,
So, time does go by,
Now I wear flat shoes with laces,
Just so I don't break my neck,
The ankles and calves look just as they are,
No illusions,
But these are,

Some Of The Things I Really Miss

Some Of The Things I Really Miss

Part 2
"All of Me"

Everything that I ever threw away or gave away,
It is rare that I don't miss each and
every item I ever possessed,
That of course says something about me
and my personality,
I treasured everything I ever received or purchased,
I have no doubt that I am a collector,
Stamps, Beanies, Videos, Books, Magazines, Clothes,
Boyd Bears, and on and on goes the list,
But now, I realize that no one else wants my "junk,"
"How dare you?"
That is not only rude, but stabs me in the heart,
I forgot about the holiday ornaments a plenty,
Who could live without them?
Probably everyone,
But, treasures are treasures,
The pirates sought them at great expense,
They gave up their lives at the very thought
of obtaining treasures,
No price was too expensive a cost,
And to this day, we have treasure and bounty hunters,
I bet every human being who lives,
wants something they do not have,
Or, to take it a step further, cannot afford,
That is one reason we have disagreements and wars,

Isn't that an interesting theory?
Let us let history check it out,
But for me, all the things I ever owned,
and no longer possess, are

Some Of The Things I Really Miss

Some Of The Things I Really Miss

―――――――――

Part 3
"My Mouth Waters at the Thought"

Ebinger's Cream Layer Cakes, Prune and Apricot Pie,
Honey Buns, Apple, Coconut Custard, Pumpkin and
Minced Thanksgiving Pies, Lemon and Lime Meringue Pies,
Danish, Lemon Roll, Breads and Rolls,
Crumb Cake, Butter Cake, Walnut and Pecan Coffee Rings,
Jelly Tarts, Stollen,
My mouth waters at the thought,

And then there were a couple of Jewish Bakeries
that I loved,
One was located on Church Avenue between
Ocean Avenue and East 18ᵗʰ Street,
The other was on Nostrand Avenue between
Glenwood Road and Flatbush Avenue,
Both were in the Borough of Brooklyn,
In New York, of course,
The Church Avenue bakery was called "Dubin's,"
Since I was very young,
and was always accompanied by an adult,
I could not tell you what their specialty was,
But I sure remember that everything
we took home with us was delicious,
I particularly liked the Jewish Rye Bread
with a pound of butter on it,
And when it became a little stale, it tasted better toasted,

24

The cakes were superb – not one was a failure,
In my mind, we could skip the main course,
Just bring on the bakery treats,
No need at my age to count the calories,
And no one even knew that cholesterol existed,
You could taste the butter
as it mingled in your mouth with the honey,
sugar, and cinnamon,
There were no chemicals then,
True flavor, true taste, true enjoyment,
My mouth waters at the thought,

When I was a teen, we moved to Nostrand Avenue,
and that bakery was called "Lord's,"
Interesting name, isn't it?
I could write a poem about "The Lord's" sweetness,

But I shant digress at this point,
We are presently immersed in decadence.
Whatever were the delights of the day in "Lords?"
Let's start with the Seven-Layered Dark
Chocolate Cake with a melt-in-your-mouth cream filling,
which held the yellow sponge cake together,
Are you with me?
Or, the honey buns that were filled with
raisins, walnuts and cinnamon,
The honey dripped from their sides
and had to be forcibly pulled from the tissue,
And all varieties of melt-in-your-mouth Danish,
Could you die?
Yes!
They featured a "Jewish Struffala" when appropriate,
The pies were outrageous, Prune and Apricot, Rhubarb
(I hated Rhubarb, but the family loved it),
I was an outcast,

The Blueberry, Peach, Plum and Five Fruit combo
cast a spell upon sight,
Some were made with a lattice top
and others opened-faced,
Can you not picture it?
To top them off, a generous
helping of real heavy whipped cream,
None of this make-believe topping of today,
Oh, I forgot each was sprinkled with powdered sugar aplenty,
It would be remiss of me not to mention all varieties
of Bobkas, Pound Cakes, and Breakfast,
"lick your fingers," sweets,
How could I have forgotten those wonderful Butter Cookies,
with nuts, caramel, and liquor sweetened dark chocolate?
My mistake,
My memory,
My mouth waters at the thought,

I forgot another bakery shop which I frequently visited
when I was very, very young, under age ten,
It was on Fifth Avenue, near 39th Street, in Brooklyn, NY,
It beckoned you, as you walked past its screened-door,
Let's see, what were my favorites?
They made the best Jelly Tarts and donuts,
Crumb Cake, Butter Cake and Coffee Rings,
Everything was made on the premises,
Apple Turnovers, Crumb and Cinnamon Buns
always topped everyone's favorite list,
And strangely enough, they made the best rolls
(Egg, Parker House and Kaiser, as I remember),
I was the one who ran to the stores in the morning,
How about seven a.m.?
Everything was fresh,
And don't think I did not cheat on the way home,
A snip of this bun or roll,

Most things at that time were packed in bags not boxes,
Easy access, you know?

And being a Brooklynite, I would be burned at the stake,
if I didn't mention "Junior's" Cheese Cake,
Again, my mouth waters at the thought,
Definitely, these are...

Some Of The Things I Really Miss

Some Of The Things I Really Miss

Part 4
"I'm Ready"

Mom's home cooking: Ziti with Sausage and Meat Balls
and Mabel's Red Sauce, Pot Roast with burnt onions,
Rib Roast with Yorkshire Pudding, Rolled Stuffed Cabbage,
Crab Meat, Shrimp and Salmon Salads,
Cole Slaw, Potato Salad, Stuffing, Fresh Ham, Tenderloin,
Lamb Roast, Spare Ribs, Baked Beans,
Vegetable Soup, Spanish rice, Macaroni and Cheese,
Tuna Casserole, Lamb Shanks, Stew,
I'm ready,

Heavy cream, butter aplenty, salt, real milk,
eggs, bacon, cold cuts (ham, Capicole, turkey,
chicken, Genoa salami, Jewish salami, bologna,
liverwurst, spiced ham, olive loaf),
cheese: Muenster, Swiss, American, Blue,
Sharp Cheddar, Hard Sharp Provolone,
Roquefort, Philadelphia Cream, Limburger,
Frankfurters,
I'm ready,

Mom's baking delights:
Pound cake, with or without raisins, Pies,
Shortbread (made with real butter), holiday cookies,
biscuits, spice cake. Hmm,
The home just reeked of goodness for days,

28

The smell of the vanilla extract,
cinnamon and all the other wonderful
ingredients permeated every room, every nostril,
Go ahead roll back the hands of time,
I'm ready,

I will never forget,
These are

Some Of The Things I Really Miss

Some Of The Things I Really Miss

Part 4A
"I'm Ready 2"

The sun rose,
It set the tone as it peeked above the rooftops,
The alarm clock pierced the morning air
with its announcement,
Get up! Get up!
The day was special and it had arrived on time,
The alarm rang an hour earlier
than it did on a workday,
That in itself, said something special
was about to happen,
It was time to prepare for the big day,
and the "The Big Bird,"
Someone had to set it "a-cookin'" –
early and slowly,
It was filled with fresh home-made stuffing
and smothered in butter,
It looked beautiful, and
within no time, it was ready to go,
"Into the oven with ya,"
Before long, the apartment was filled
with the most wonderful "smell,"
Oh, all right, "aroma,"
It filled every corner of every room,
In fact, it filled every nostril of
those present, including the cat,

He was walking around with his nose
in the air, twitching like a rabbit's,
"Frisky" loved "Big Bird," and knew
that treats would be "a-comin'" soon,
Mom prepared the victuals,
As the cooking steam created running water
on the windows,
It spoke of the cold outdoors,
But we had it beat,
We were warm
inside and out, body and spirit,
I finished the dusting,
vacuuming, and setting the Holiday table,
Company is coming,
The bird is being basted, and oh, boy,
does it smell sweet and deeeelicious,
The dressing is particularly good –
simple, but "out-of-this-world,"
A dry dressing made with homemade
dried bread crumbs, fresh onions
and celery, salt and pepper,
and a hint of "Poultry Seasoning,"
I drool,
And can't wait for the "tasty" morsels
to caress my taste buds – Hmmmm,
Just thinking about placing a small piece of crispy
skin on my tongue makes me jump with joy,
"That's got to be the best,"
I was ready,

The apartment was ready,
Mom was ready,
However, the "The Tom" was still doing his thing,
You just can't rush "deeelicious!"
Besides, the company had not arrived yet,

I guessed that it would be polite to wait for them,
I wished that they would hurry up,
I was being tantalized to death,
Iris, Bob, Linda and Cindy had to stop to
pick up Lois, and her Mom, Aggie,
Aunt Net and Uncle Bill were coming
by taxi (tough to get on a Holiday),
My brother, Jackie,
walked from his apartment house to ours,
And my Mom and I were bumping into each other,
trying to get all the last minute stuff ready,
You know,
the usual serving dishes, extra-large spoons,
knives, special dishes for the rolls and bread, and desserts,
The pies looked lush, Ebinger's best,
Well, I have to leave you now; the doorbell just rang,
I wonder who will be first?
You'll never know,
Because this is just one day in a lifetime,
repeated for many years, however,
But, it unequivocally tells you,
why these precious moments still live,
and are held close,
Just…

Some Of The Things I Really Miss

Dotty's Christmas Party

The year was 1969,
The time was Christmas,
The place was one of my dear associate,
Dotty's, apartment,
It was located in a lovely section of Brooklyn
called "The Heights,"
She was giving her first Holiday party
in her new home,
She invited some of her new neighbors,
And my mom, my brother, Jack, and I,
plus three close friends, Iris and Bob and Lois,
Dotty was a "love," a regular fun person,
We all were delighted,
and could not wait for the big event,
A few days before the big event, she seemed
to have some trepidation about our attending,
Dotty knew we could be "hell-raisers,"
However, she felt better because
my mom would be with us,
That helped,
Dotty somehow felt we were up to something,
Her final words to Iris and me Friday
evening as we left the office were...
"See you tomorrow night –
Just behave, don't embarrass me,"
Oh, my...we chuckled,
She was right,
She and her new neighbors

were in for a surprise,
We all decided to dress up "special"
for the occasion,
My mom was a good sport,
She dressed up as "Mamma Cass,"
She wore an old (but clean) pink Chenille bedspread
and a handmade Indian beaded belt around her forehead.
She carried a long, long, long cigarette holder
and strummed a Ukulele,
For her efforts she later suffered a bout of pneumonia,
After all, she had to change in the staircase
of the apartment on a bitter cold winter's night,
In fact, it snowed all day,

I was dressed in a black
silk-flowered printed dressing gown,
And in order to keep warm,
I wore a long plaid,
red woolen scarf with 3" fringe
and a matching large red pom-pom beret,
Classy to say the least,

My brother fit right in,
He wore black-stained trousers
tied with a rope-belt,
The white jacket and front-only collared shirt
that held the red large-flowered tie
set everything off perfectly,
It didn't end there,
He topped it off with large-black heavy-rimmed,
lenses less glasses
and a 1940's gray fedora hat to keep his head warm,
That was my family,

Bob, Iris' husband, opted to remain "normal,"

"Oh, pooooh,"
But, Iris and Lois, my buddies, were fully decked out,

Lois was my brother's "date,"
She wore a black-lace toilet seat cover
over a long, curled blonde wig,
A long white skirt with a yellow beer-can
emblazoned on a cut-off sleeve
sweatshirt with baked-on rhinestone roses (gorgeous),
Under the skirt she wore cotton long johns
with red knee-high socks,

Ah, the pièce-de-résistance, Iris,
She was very tall and wore a brown wool skirt
short enough to show off her
oversized, pink rayon half-thigh panties,
She piled her hair high with curls
and decorated that creation with tiny,
colorful Christmas tree balls,
Of course, there were several dangling,
varying length rope necklaces,
and a yellow feathered boa nestled on a purple top,

It didn't end there,
What's a party without music?
We created posters and banners,
and parodies on some crazy old tunes
to fit the occasion,
In those outfits how could we possibly make
a grand entrance without music?
We marched down the hall from the elevator
to Dotty's apartment
carrying all the signs and singing,
We knew we would not disturb the neighbors;
they were at the party,

We sat on the floor and sang, and sang,
            Not, my mom,
      Mamma Cass changed clothes,
            and sat on a chair,
      After our show, we were introduced
            to Dotty's new neighbors,
I must say, "They seemed somewhat speechless,"
Oh well, everyone agreed, we had a great time,
      And I guess, particularly me,
            since I have such recall,
Forty-seven years later these memories remain,

      Can you believe these antics were not
            the highlight of the night for me?
      No, there was one tender moment that
            stole the memory show,
            Because it was Christmas,
      everyone insisted that I sing the *"Ave Maria,"*
      I was sitting opposite my mom,
            looking right at her as I sang,
I watched the tears of joy flow down her face,
      I finished the solo to stop the flow,
The love shown me in that moment remains
            one of the strongest in my life,
      It is mine, and will remain so – forever.

A note for my readers:
Remember, when tears flow they sometimes
find their way into your forever "brook of life."

Back Stage

'The Day I Ran Away'

Have you ever been backstage
in a theatre on Broadway?
I have, and it took my breath away,
I went to an open audition,
dressed in gingham and ready to sing,
This babe in Toyland did not know a thing,
Who came prepared with music of their choice?
Who had credits praising their voice?
Oh, my, look at those 8" x 10" glossies
in black and white,
And there I stood naked alright,
I did everything I could for appearance sake,
But, after hearing all the excitement, seeing agents and
portfolios, I felt I was at my own wake,
The 3" x 5" index card was the best,
'Name, address, telephone number and your experience;
you know the rest!'
'I do? Not by a long shot, fella,'
If someone touched me at that moment,
I would be self-propelled without a propeller,
I was so nervous; I thought I would die,
I kept looking to the heavens, asking, 'Why?'
But I knew why, I wanted my life to be changed,
Sitting in a 1916 marbled Bank corner
typing, smacks of being 'deranged,'
So here I am, supposedly in a dentist chair –

just a little white lie,
Desperately wanting to sing on a Broadway stage;
my 'pie-in-the sky,'
And, if it wasn't for some fine mature applicant
in front of me, I would still be in the street,
There I stood with one 3" x 5" card; no music, no glossies,
no credits, no agent, being most discreet,
Call attention to myself, not right now;
thank God, she broke the ice,
She was so very sweet, caring – simply nice,
She asked, "Are you having problems
filling out the card?"
"No, not really," for me, it wasn't that hard,

She shared her black and white photos with pride,
And all her experience – more than a mile wide,
She had her music, rolled neat and ready to go,
"Have you no music, or pictures;" I replied, "No,"
I noticed she left out credits, no need to explain,
She was being polite; the reason was plain,
She asked again, if she might help me to fill out
my 3" x 5" card, showing me what she had done,
At that point, while still outside, I should have run,
But the line kept inching along,
What surprised me was that no one burst into song,
The excitement swelled as we
moved closer to the stage door,
By the way before I forget, I had one entry on the card;
30 years choir experience – no more,
But the job was to join a choral group – be a nun,
In the "Sound of Music;" it was having a wonderful run,
I just stepped beyond the stage door entrance ledge,
No time to hesitate; no time to hedge,
My head said, "You have come this far, go on,"
Two to go on stage before me;

then it will be over and I'll be gone,
A voice from the darkened theatre yelled,
"Two bars and a high 'C,'"
My God, I don't know if I can sing a high 'C,'
So naïve, I couldn't read a note,
but wanted to sing on Broadway,
It had been such a wonderful experience;
such a wonderful day,
But at that point I ran; I handed my
3" x 5" card to the "Stagedoor Manager," as I flew by,
To this day, I can still hear him yelling –
"Don't go, don't go, at least try,"
He was right; I later found out that
I could sing much higher than a high 'C,'
I guess Broadway really was not for me,
If only I knew what I was doing;
I should have at my age,
At least I got to see the props as I waited my turn

Back Stage

*(How about a 'B' above high 'C,' that was
actually the top of my range)*

39

Time To Move On

I looked up to make a wish
out my car door,
I was waiting for some wicked,
billowy clouds to thaw,
They were ready to spread
some nasty stones of ice,
But they sat silent as they threatened;
remained quite nice,
They put on a lovely
picturesque show of naughty – tough,
They were somewhere else
down the road becoming rough,
Not a squeak, not a chill, not a sound,
They in their magnificence, simply rolled around,
Casting an omen; giving a strong warning,
Watch what you do; I have the whole day –
it is still morning,
So as I drove I watched and
wondered what they might have in mind,
Then they moved on; the sky returned to blue
and became gentle and kind,
The threat was over; it was gone,
When those billowy beasts of beauty,
decided ...

Time To Move On

In The Chair

Years ago when my mother was alive,
It was customary to watch TV after dinner;
relax, it was after five,
Dishes were washed and put away;
then I had homework to do,
It seemed as though I was always in school,
never through,
But my mother, God love her,
kept the apartment top notch,
Laundry, and shopping, and cooking –
she deserved a little TV watch,
Funny thing, just as it is true for me today,
she would fall asleep,
Almost instantly, the snores would come –
no conversation – not a peep,
And on occasion, she would wake and wonder
what happened to her favorite show,
Well, I would fill her in,
and along to bed she would go,
Like a sleeping pill,
the "boob-tube" did its thing,
She was well on her way on Mr. Sandman's wing,
How odd; I guess it had something to do with age,
She worked part-time in a local retail shop;
certainly not for the wage,
To get out of the house and
buy me some beautiful clothes,
To be active; get away from her own inner woes,

But that too stopped one day,
when she thwarted a crook,
Locked the door, just before he tried to get in,
but she was shook,
She never went back,
even though she enjoyed that time,
It wasn't worth her life to earn another dime,
So, she occupied her days making clothes for me,
Never complained, never seemed to worry about
tomorrow and what would be,
She was happy; yet, she was not,
How bored she must have been –
dying of human dry rot,
I gave her credit though,
She always looked just so,
She was not a spender, that was for sure,
She budgeted well; we never wanted for anything –
we were not rich, not poor,
Rich in spirit, not financially well-to-do,
Every so often, she'd splurge;
have her hair done – 'whoopee-doo,'
She'd even give that up, if I had a need,
Her children, my brother and I,
came first, yes, indeed,
And now although she has been gone many years
from our planet Earth,
I hope she received a just reward;
one equal to her worth,
And I hope too, that she is somehow aware,
That it is now my turn,
to watch TV and fall asleep…

In The Chair

? ? ? ? ? A Dream Is A Dream, Is A Dream

Strange as it may seem,
I dream, and dream, and dream,
People visit who are long gone from the scene,
And sometimes, oh, how I want them to stay,
But they just fade with little or nothing to say,
There are times I am most grateful for the visit,
But I wish
they would have been a little more revealing and explicit,
The latest was my brother, who was not long gone,
But still questioning my love from the great beyond,
We were both traveling on a bus
but he got off before me,
He did the same in life;
and if I judge it right, he is now happy to be free,
In my view, life for him was always a trauma;
hard for him to handle, understand,
It seemed to me the love he sought in life,
he found in animal land,
In the unconditional love of all the pets he owned,
And they too, were in reality, simply loaned,
He wanted the love he could not give or find,
Asking I'm sure, "Is everyone blind?"
He seemed to have a need no one could fill,
And even in the end
no one was there, when he was so ill,
Maybe in his present state,

he has finally found a more peaceful daily tide,
But I know he dreams of the day when his
"Pek Tommy" will once again walk by his side,
Even in death, I feel we will dream,
Perhaps hidden shadows will be revealed in Eternity's gleam,
But for now, whether day or night, dark or bright...

A Dream Is A Dream, Is A Dream ? ? ? ? ?

The Bracelet

The year – 1951,
The gift – a sterling silver linked, charm bracelet,
The occasion – Grammar School Graduation,
The charm – a diploma
The gift giver – a lovely neighbor,
Mrs. Rybecki, (2nd floor left),
Today – 2017,
The gift is still in use,
But, the diploma is no longer alone,
Many other charms have been added,
Each with their own memories;
each holding tight to their links,
Sentimental,
Beyond belief,
A biography on a wrist,
Charming moments of laughter and joy,
The diploma was just a start of future events,
Each new charm denoting a special experience
a special moment in my life,
Thank you to a dear friend and neighbor,
One to be remembered forever

Write What You See

A few lines are just as good as none,
When you write daily and profess, "Every day
some writing must be done,"
There are so many things that cry – "Look at me,"
That of course makes it easy to write what you see,

Look at a chair, its shape – its color – its size,
Question who did rest their bum – dull, or wise?
Guaranteed over its lifetime, children to aged all took a turn,
Rested upon its seat so strong and firm,
Many weary bones were thankful for that treat,
Finding rest upon its welcoming seat,

On, and on, this story could flow,
Why not ask, "Where did the wood in its frame grow?"
Who might be the first to bring it home?
Who would decide which room it should grace,
and when it should roam?
Might it become a dust collector in an attic for years?
Then suddenly emerge as a wonderful memory
with some sentimental tears?,
What about that attic time? Was it not filled with
life stories – deep mystery?
Didn't it have so much to give, wonderful history?
I'll bet millions of tales to tell,
Enough for any imagination to run pell-mell,
"Why is it where it is today?"
"Was it sold or simply given away?"

Before it was discarded, did it turn like humans, to dust?
By the way, no one ever asked whether it was caned,
cushioned or metal, left to age and rust.

Whatever, I will end this saga with a challenge for each of you,
Find your creative glow, capture what you
see for posterity and follow through,
Writing is so exciting and simple, if you just try; follow me,
Look at the World, the Universe, Life, and…write, yes write,

Write What You See

Your Fantastic Butter Tub

Oh, we are so smug,
As we snuggle like "bugs in a rug,"
We live our lives in a manner sweet,
In places and ways built by hearts and hands
of others we will never know, or meet,
We didn't build the bridges,
or lay railroad tracks,
Pour tar and concrete for roads
and streets without cracks,
Create beautiful buildings and parks,
We had nothing to do with
the past generation's marks,
Each generation sits its bottom in the
previous generation's butter tub,
Now couldn't that always be a rub?
As we enjoy their work from the sweat
of their brows; relax in their bathtub,
Think about that tub;
the next time you rub-a-dub, and scrub,
I wonder who created that wonderful
convenience in which we bathe,
Dunking without any thought of by
whom it might have been made,
That is just a given, and aren't we blessed?
Think of all the "little" things;
the absence of which, would put us to the test,
Running water, a car, locks,
electricity, heat to name but a few,

Without them today, whatever would we do?
So many who came before us,
created many a novel thing,
We are the fortunate recipients of what their
mind's treasures did bring,
Will we when we join their ranks,
be able to truly say, "Move over 'bub,'"
I added to your efforts, I just didn't wallow in...

Your Fantastic Butter Tub

What More Could I Ask?

Today is one and one-half hours old,
I'm reflecting on yesterday's moments,
now growing old,
The warmth and pleasures
were too numerous to note,
Beginning with breakfast at the beach
with a friend; on that I could dote,
The sun was warm;
the breeze off the sound, brisk,
And spending quality time with a friend
is always tops on my list,
The fresh air and sun wore me down,
believe it or not,
And I looked at all the papers in my house
and wished they would rot,
The chipmunks were out in force running
around, scurrying here and there,
Running from humans who
were out in force everywhere,
I run from most humans too;
they are up to no good,
Busy trying to check out your plans,
your life, if they could,
'It is not winter,
why do you have on a coat and hat?'
'My business,' but I would never say that,
I did explain how cool it was at the shore,
Then I was happy to move on,

go in and close my door,
As much as I enjoy people,
I enjoy my solitude too,
Enjoy quietly thinking my thoughts,
while doing what I want to do,
Taking care of my sweet little cat,
who is not well,
Wishing she could understand that
I think she's tops – swell,
And then, a simple call from another friend,
Catching up on some news –
How many cards I have to send,
Working on the computer, recording
my daily poems which have been written,
but not recorded to date,
I like to keep them current; that cannot wait,
Before I know it, the day is gone,
But it was one with some nice warm
memories to look back upon,
And now it is past time to say "goodnight;"
another day is taking off its mask,
But yesterday,
I had some sweet moments of joy –

What More Could I Ask?

Lost Without You

⸺⸺⸺⸺❦⸺⸺⸺⸺

(Samantha Cali, My Sweet Calico Cat)

Oh, my little friend,
I am lost without you,
I see you everywhere I do,
I hated to leave you at the vet,
I bet you miss me too, my pet,
Cali, you are missed;
I missed fixing your dinner tonight,
And hearing you jump after a short flight,
No meows,
no purring to warm my soul,
No beautiful eyes checking me out
in my 'mommy' role
I could not brush, and wash,
and pet you, as I do each day,
I missed that; I must say,
Please get well soon, so I
can hold you tight
And feel you close under the cover at night,
You are very special, my friend;
please come back soon, please do,
So I can tell you how much you
were missed, and how much I was…

Lost Without You

Samantha

Samantha, why do you want to leave?
If you go, I will so sorely grieve,
My heart is breaking, watching you go downhill,
Drinking more and more; seeing you become more still,
You are so young, when compared to my prior feline love,
I wonder why you're being called away; who is calling from above?
Why are they so intent on stealing you away?
Oh, how I will miss you so each night and day,
This has to be one of the cruelest things in life to endure,
To see a lovely, faithful animal suffer without a cure,
Every part of you has been checked, and A-OK'd,
And yet, you have lost your way, even with all the aid,
I don't want to let you go,
But it seems to be your wish, you know?
I can't even pick you up and hold you anymore,
You are too heavy and feel pain,
even when moving on the floor,
Science has failed us, my pet,
But there is one thing on which you can bet,
I will not let you suffer for my sake,
I will just accept whatever the call;
let my heart break,
And so it will, my little friend,
And be it known, you'll
have my love far beyond the end,
There comes a time when we all must part,
And usually,
it means another break in the heart,

When love is shared, who wants to leave?
And for one remaining,
what is left, but to grieve,
But when you get to your final rest
on the home side,
The welcome will be warm
as the gate swings wide,
You have done quite a job in filling that need,
Certainly my little friend you did succeed,
Time for you to be pain free,
Time for you to be as you wish to be,
Time for you to roam unharmed
in fields of clover,
To once again breathe fresh air
and the fragrance of flowers all over,
You were well fed and groomed,
protected from harm,
But a prisoner without the
freedom of the wild – a farm,
But never forget me please,
I tried my best,
And I hope when we meet again, you'll invite me
to be your guest,
To feel your warmth and hear you purr,
And see you as you should be,
healthy as you once were,
God bless my little love,
I am sure He will in His abode above,
I will bring your remains back with me,
when I get my call,
And hopefully you'll meet
my other wee-friends in the Hallowed Hall,
Love and licks and kisses will abound,
For what was lost will be found,
We will all be introduced, reunited,

each with a mended broken heart,
Unconditional forgiveness, love, true contentment;
together again never to part,
Yes, we will be as we were; I'll hear your purr,
All my love to you, my sweet

Samantha

For That I'll Roam

"Each age has its genius,"
so it is said,
But for me, the greatest genius
rests with the dead,
We all travel far and wide to enjoy
the creations of those long gone,
We see, we feel, we enjoy,
and create memories to lean upon,
But today, what genius
makes me want to leave home?
There is nothing like
'The Pieta,' 'St. Peter's Square' with
Cellini's 'Matchless Colonnade,' in Rome,
That's indescribable beauty –
creation at its best,
Add Seneca, Socrates, Sophocles – minds
running bold and wild – Do their souls rest?
Keats, Yeats, Shakespeare,
also come to mind,
To feel the presence of their spirit
where they live, I find,
To stand beneath Michelangelo's art in the
Sistine Chapel; to feel the love, the hate,
They all gave their lives for the craft
they loved to share…to create,
And now though dead, they live on forever,
And I want to feel their spirits,
the flowing inspiration in each endeavor,

What have we today?
Stark buildings and bridges,
and things that make me want to stray,
To go back and absorb the
creative genius of the dead,
My thoughts are my thoughts;
I have passion for what I've said,
Where are the Beethovens, Strauss',
Chopins, Bachs and Mozarts of our age?
Oh, there is room for 'bee-bop,' 'hard rock,'
'rap,' foul moments on stage,
But there is no great genius, no class,
Much of today's creation is based solely on crass,
A dot in the middle of a white canvas
is accepted as art,
It lacks so badly of beauty, realism;
it's no better than the proverbial gale's fart,
No substance, no heart, no depth of soul,
No understanding of an everlasting gift;
no, that's not the goal,
And so,
down through the ages to be different,
changes have been made,
But, they have come and gone
and live in the land of fade,
And on we go, in search of the beauty of the past,
Because it speaks to our whole being;
its message was made to last,
I have touched upon, but a few, of antiquity's gems,
The one's critics still review with other items,
How insulting can we be?
It is easy to challenge the dead, interpret
their value, their worth; my advice, 'go create a tree,'
All the past geniuses rise above,
but their spirits hover near,

They are what they wanted to become,
that is quite clear,
They were blessed with
something beyond our reach,
The spirit of all creation instilled in them
the powers to silently preach and teach,
They touched the ultimate joy found in art,
and so it was recorded,
If we would only take the time to feel their pain and emotions;
we would understand their creations were delivered as ordered,
By a power unknown to most who walk the earth,
Because the hand of God touched their souls at birth,
Give me yesterday's genius;
for we in their shadows are fools and jesters,
We don't think about living down through the ages;
no, self-interest festers,
What makes me want to leave home?
The creations of the geniuses; those that last forever...

For That I'll Roam

That Hollow World, Ever Echoing

It is a hollow world, when those you knew
and loved are all gone,
But their life's sweet melody remains; it lingers on,
Their memories flow like a wonderful old flick,
Birthdays, holidays, special events, like many a picnic,
Joys and sorrows, shared laughter and tears,
Then suddenly, you find yourself standing alone,
facing all those years,
Family, friends, associates,
each one fills a hand-picked picture frame,
You look at them; they smile back,
they seem to be calling your name,
And each of those moments finds its place in time,
A thought of that snapped second, makes you giggle,
and your spirits climb,
Immediately,
it brings you back into their lives... Wow!
To wonder perhaps, what might they be doing now?
Whether alive, or resting beyond your reach,
their spirits live on,
They are living an eternal life within you,
even though they are gone,
You can find comfort, warmth,
a quiet joy forever beckoning,
In that mysterious place,

That Hollow World, Ever Echoing

My Sled

There it stood, lonely, against the barn wall,
It stood clean, and waiting, leaning tall,
We had a grand, steep, bump less hill,
And as we rode,
the laughs grew louder with each passing spill,
I picture once more,
my mom's and dad's joy for me,
As they watched and listened
for my greatest glee,
Each ride made the hill steeper and
faster with the snow now packed tight,
And at night from my window,
the moon recalled with me, the day's delight,
The sled once again leaned against the barn wall,
It was proud, and clean, and dry; it stood tall,
It had waited quietly for a long time this year,
before it felt the cold, fluffy white,
and heard the children cheer,
As their little bellies flopped upon its slats of wood,
Sinking the blades flat to gather the speed,
they knew it could,
My friends and I,
with faces, cheeks and noses bright red,
Patiently waited for the cold,
the excitement upon which we all fed,
Our mittens were wet right down to the skin,
But not one would think of running home, or stepping in,
A dry pair of mittens was not on anyone's mind,

Just all the fun and joy of a snowfall of this kind,
In between rides, snowballs flew,
We were children to the core, and we knew what to do,
Back to the sled, time and time again,
faster and faster, down the hill it sped,
That motor less wonder; that old reliable, "Flexible Flyer,"

My Sled

Sister Jeanette? Wanna Bet?

"Have you ever been a nun?"
My co-workers did not inquire or ask
that question to make fun,
They would corner me and say,
"Have you ever been a nun?"
My reply, "Of course, many times,"
That was my usual quip
with a comment about chimes,
I could never figure out why
they asked me, to be frank,
For they all knew I always worked in a bank,
Perhaps it was something I said at one time;
perhaps something I did, or do,
I must have projected a very angelic view,
Maybe it was because I never used curse words,
Instead of saying, "shit," I would substitute, "turds,"
But, "Are you a nun?" struck a chord,
At that time, it was out of
character for me, possibly an unearned reward,
Or, was it? Little did they know!
In prior years, I went to seven o'clock mass,
religiously, rain, sleet, or snow,
Every morning, I would find my way to my knees,
At the altar, in beautiful St. Michael's Church,
if you please,
My heart was full of faith; I had a firm belief,
But my family wanted no part of that,
much to my grief,

I was only seven or eight years of age,
Nowhere near a true time of reason, unable to self-gage,
So, my life was changed by the adults around,
Their way was after all, totally sound,
Today, my friend, Mary,
reminded me of my co-workers on the Anchor set,
When she asked, "Do you remember when they
used to call you, 'Sister Jeanette'?"
I do not think she ever knew about them asking,
"Have you ever been a nun?"
And even after I assured them, it was not
part of my prior life, the term "Sister" had begun,
No matter what I said, they didn't believe me,
I told them, "They would not have me;"
too many dirty jokes and "habits," you see,
My co-workers simply wanted me to be
a nun; "Get the net,"

Sister Jeanette? Wanna Bet?

True Friends

My mother had pneumonia and I was on the verge of same,
The doctor came to the house; he actually came,
He left a prescription for my mom and another for me,
But the Drug Store was pretty far away;
it was snowy, bitter cold, near '0' degree,
My first contact for help, gave a negative response –
loud and clear,
"Not in this weather, my, dear,"
The buses were nowhere to be found,
It was treacherous on any roadbed ground,
Taxis were at a premium, if running at all,
All you got was a busy signal, when you gave a call,
But when my friend, Lois, gave a buzz, and heard about our plight,
she said she'd pick up the prescriptions and have them filled,
She walked from her house to ours – a couple of miles;
boy, she was strong-willed,
Then she walked another five or six avenue blocks to the store,
I called to make sure they would be opened, 'Just until 8 p.m.,
not a minute more,
The weather is bad and we all have to get home,'
I understood, but I was fearsome,
My friend still had not reached our place,
And when she arrived, there was little time to chat; she had to
keep up her pace,
They were locking up, when she got to the store,
They knew what she had done and who she was;
they opened the door,
Talk about angels, true friends;

these are the things you do not forget,
She was special, loving and kind, and the first to pass, I regret,
We got our medicine, and she walked back home,
How can one ever pay such a debt, for effort maximum; I
could write a tome,
One of our own turned us down,
All show, man of the town,
He always felt hurt and abused,
But he did so little; others he used,
So Lois, you still hold a high place in memory and heart,
My Mother and I never forgot what you did;
you set yourself far apart,

I should be as generous as you,
In life, there are many 'friends;'
but like you, few,
And I was blest; I had another couple
who were angels to the core,
Had they known,
they would have gone to the store,
My best friend, Iris and her husband, Bob,
Iris passed away in 1999;
she suffered, reason enough to sob,
Bob and I still remained friends;
saw each other twice a year,
Our lives intertwined for over fifty years;
each moment treasured and dear,
Our tears and laughter, interwove,
as our lives moved on,
They changed many times, but we shared
the love friends give, and we can depend upon,
Most times support;
they always knew how to give,
But as with all things in life, the tether stretches
wide; they found another way to live,

So as time moved on,
others filled their need and thought,
We still remained close in heart, but many
times to each other we were an afterthought,
Their needs changed;
mine remained the same,
Their children grew, expanded,
moved away; their world was aflame,
I was stuck in mud; most times unable to go,
I could not travel, or put on any good show,
My entertainment days fell to none,
And the trio dwindled – each, as one,
In other words, by circumstance,
we went our own way,
'But where's the love and friendship,
the lifelong bond, you say?'
It is in the mind and heart;
it never ends,
There are many called 'friends;' but few
are revered and remembered forever as …

True Friends

The Silent

Family & Friends

The silent piano,

The silent guitar,

The silent voices,

NOT OF THEIR CHOOSING, BUT LIFE'S!

REMEMBER,

The Silent

Behavior As Taught, Behavior As Learned

'O, resident of the womb, before you arrive,
you know how to behave, how to grow,
Who was your first teacher,
do you happen to know?'
Once released, you have new trainers;
who might they be?
Mom, dad, and anyone else, whomever you see,
Your learning begins anew,
You must learn how, what, and when to do,
Proper behavior is instituted immediately;
universally societal from breath one,
You know what to do,
and when you are done,
Your olfactory system plays a role,
You are being trained on a bowl,
With rewards you quickly learn,
This is the way to go; this is a new turn,
And so, your behavior is in a constant
state of change,
It is just the start of a much longer,
wider and broader range,
Now you've got the drift, what I am talking about,
How dare you pout!
Behavior is taught; behavior is learned,
Rewards are given, sometimes, even earned,
We are all classic mimics – our lives,

their essence – sheer mimicry,
There are few who can show cause to disagree,
Even with a world full of available options,
Our choices are mainly a matter of adoptions,
All our ways in life are at best, what
we have been taught,
Too few if ever, ride the star they, only they, have caught,
Not only ride the 'whirligig,'
but watched it as it turned,
Life is 'ne plus ultra,' … perfect,
but most succumb to a lifetime of…

Behavior As Taught, Behavior As Learned

It's Temporary, It 'Tis

Each place in which we live is temporary
you see,
Even our time on *Earth*
is a short trip upon any open sea,
We journey from place to place,
We stop and fill a home – a special space,
Then, most times, we move on,
We find another spot to fill and rest upon,
And in each place,
we leave part of our spirit behind,
And too, as we go, we carry part
of each place in our mind,
Memories of a particular view,
a quiet corner, a special spot,
No matter how far away we roam, we hold
those thoughts – and say, 'I never forgot,'
For me, each place holds a part of me
and those I love,
Many of whom have already
returned home above,
The memory of home,
wherever it might be, is what it is,
But we will always remember our
journey on *Earth;* even though

It's Temporary, It 'Tis

Yesterday

Everyone professed to be 'religious,'
What did that mean?
That they had faith?
Or, that they attended church services regularly?
Perhaps they prayed daily,
Prayed what?
Repeated the prayers of others,
Prayed repetitively?
That was not me; I prayed repetitiously,
Some prescribed prayers and some prayers/thoughts of my own,
And very often I prayed that God would
forgive me my "mundaneness,"
But there was one thing I did not do,
I did not worship those who had the privilege of entertaining me,
I learned a long time ago that there was but One in charge,
And it was not me,
When I grew up, we as a family had little,
We of course, considered ourselves 'Middle Class,'
What was that?
We weren't poor,
No, there were others who lived in greater need,
We weren't rich,
There were those who had much more than we,
And when there was a need, we helped each other,
Family, friends, and neighbors shared as best they could,
Not everyone owned a house,
Not every family, let alone each member of
each family, owned a car,

Designer clothes were unheard of,
'Hand-me-downs,' were the rage,
the 'designer clothes' of the day,
Designer sneakers - they were unheard of,
Sneakers were for gym class,
They weren't worn on the street,
Unless you were really poor and couldn't afford
a good pair of shoes,
No, times have surely changed,
I remember the excitement of getting a new pair of shoes,
And that was once, or at max, twice a year,
It was a must for the beginning of the school year,
At Easter you would get a beautiful new
outfit, including new shoes,
hat, gloves, coat, pocketbook, hankie, etc.; how lovely,
My brother got a new suit, shoes and a hat,
And everyone else lived that same scene,
It was lovely on Easter morning to gather at church
and check everyone out,
It wasn't so lovely to have fallen because of the slippery
soles on new shoes,
That often happened,
Or to suffer the blisters on heels, because of a poor fit,
Patent leather was the call of the day,
And Vaseline was the polish agent,
I remember a wonderful shoe store on
Atlantic Avenue, called 'Cowards,'
They had the best, long-lasting shoes,
Thick soles, sturdy laces, good arch support and no style,
Oh, maybe the style of the day,
'Bucks,' loafers and saddle shoes were the in thing,
Wow!
My brother went to Florsheim's Shoe Store,
Not much choice...color,
but no style or designer-wear,

But somehow, we all survived,
And, we were none the worse for wear,
Were we upset, psychologically?
I would venture a guess that we
nor our parents, knew the word,
Psychologically speaking, psychology didn't exist,
At least not in our circles,
If you had a problem,
you were simply told to 'get over it,'
And, so you did,
Negatives were not emphasized,
Money was never a problem,
There was little to be had,
Extra's? There was no such thing,
How about this for a treat?
A tiny cup of some sugar candy with a
tiny spoon (that made it last longer),
Here's one for the books,
My mother would have died to know this one,
I used to go to one of the local bar windows,
and ask patrons for pretzels,
I hung out there, because the place had
the smoothest sidewalk for roller-skating,
And the bar room windows were always
opened in the summer,
To this day, I can smell the beer on the bar room floor,
However did we survive?
The smells of the neighborhood – that was home,
The local park – open space and the fragrances
of the seasons – that was home,
The smell of the chlorine from the pool in summer,
And the locker room on the way in and out of the pool area,
The smell of the gas and oil,
as I strolled through the local gas station,
Oh, it was a short-cut,

The smell of burning coal and coal deliveries,
And a piece of coal was priceless – Black Chalk,
Sleigh-riding in winter, roller skating,
bike riding (if you had a bike), and swimming in summer,
Oh, yes, thank God for the local P.A.L.
They had organized activities – free,
Speaking of free, that was the key to our entertainment,
Early on Saturdays, we would go to the local movies,
It cost three-cents for the children's show,
We saw two-full-length features, a cartoon,
a serial (without ending),
Movie Tone News and up-coming movie previews,
The serials were the week-to-week draw,
Since the end was never an end,
it was always, 'to be continued,'
So, you know we all had to return the following week,
Candy was one to five-cents per box,
There was enough candy to last the whole show,
And if you were conservative,
you would have some left to take home,
Ah, the adults, the best were the 'Matrons,'
They were for 'mob' control,
God bless them,
They had their hands full,
Once seated, you couldn't change seats,
And "no talking" – Oh, no!
They had huge flashlights that blinded you,
when they would shine the light into your eyes,
One infraction – okay,
The second you were led out the door,
Every now and again the huge side door would open,
Someone was sneaking in – or, being escorted out,
But the sunlight lit up the whole area,
And depending upon which door,
it might fade the motion picture on the screen,

When that happened, you had to hear the deafening screams,
It was all just a wonderful experience – for kids,
Oh, the best, you had to be led to the bathroom
and back…one at a time,
Need I say more?
We all had terrific retention powers,
Saturday mornings at the movies, were the best,
You were left with not only something to remember,
but something to look forward to,
Movies were actually one of the main forms of entertainment,
The best were the nights when they gave away free things,
mostly dinnerware – to keep you coming back,
They distributed dinner plates,
tea cups, saucers, and dessert dishes, etc.
But before you left the theater,
it was a must that you purchase some War Bond Stamps,
I remember having my own book for ten cent stamps,
I think my Mom's book was for twenty-five cent stamps,
Yes that was patriotic, a must,
But for us kids, we all looked forward to
Saturday mornings at the movies,
We were there for hours and when
we left the theater – whoa, that light!
It was blinding, brighter than bright,
That's what happens after
spending so much time in the dark,
But, happy we were ~ more than happy,
What a wonderful life!
That was …

Yesterday

Reflections

The day after any day is a day of 'Reflections,'
In other words ~ serious thought ~
recollected perceptions,
Forget it! That's an act of futility,
Bordering on absurdity,
You cannot unsay what has been said;
undo what has been done,
What has been lost, cannot be won,
So, let the day after be what it is ~ brand new,
The slate clean;
time to let time run its course through,
Question is; will it be a day of perfections?
Or, will tomorrow, as most days after are,
be filled with memories and …

Reflections

Long Life And Too Much
Water Under The Bridge

If we stay around – live long enough,
Lots of things go up in a puff,
Actually they float on by, irretrievable,
like water under the bridge,
To have captured the moment
might have been most rewarding – a privilege,
But once the moment has fled,
what can we say – not much – just smile instead ~
Life goes on; new days replace the old,
Memories of lost moments embellish stories now told,
Stories about what could have been,
if we had been more wise,
Let the water that trickles through the fingers
rest where it lies,
For there will always be regrets, water over the ridge,
And if we are lucky enough to survive, we will know...

Long Life And Too Much
Water Under The Bridge

The Role Played By Fate
'TITANIC REASONS? OR, JUST ONE?'

The month was April; the day the 15th; the year 1912,
The beginning of a story into which the world
would never cease to delve,
the subject - a giant, unsinkable ship, that sank,
Killing 1502 without regard of social and world rank,
The frozen waters of the North Atlantic became
an instant mausoleum to house unbelieving souls,
As 705 survivors sang, and prayed,
and mourned their brave, sacrificial idols,
Who would ever believe this story to be true?
It is so fantastic, it smacks of fantasy through and through,
It is 84 years later, and the world still, for answers longs,
Who can be labeled,
who is the demon responsible for all the wrongs?
And so, like many disasters and wars,
someone must take the blame,
Someone must pay, be put to shame,
That could be quite the case,
But it is not – blame does not always find a face,
The reasons were multiple and titanic, to say the least,
But not the true nature of that beast,
Man's inability to ignore a dangerous challenge, or threat,
Publicly expressed, blowing his own trumpet,
Monsieur Ismay, what did you do?
Demanding a half-empty lifeboat be lowered away;
a lifeboat numbering one of too few,
And so you saved yourself,

and lived a labeled life of shame,
For your life was over – never, and rightly so, the same,
Lifeboats – greed –
wanting to show the world, who is the best,
It was all superfluous, means nothing,
when 1502 souls go to their Eternal Rest,
It was right that you chose to live,
You were not worthy to be counted among those
who died, as they did,
To pay the ultimate sacrifice for others misdeeds,
Represents a far greater glory than a
coward's ultimate needs,
But, when all is said and done,
And investigations exhaust their findings one-by-one,
Answers rest in the one vacuum housing all
unresolved historical moments to date,
No one can deny, with any certainty...

The Role Played By Fate
'TITANIC REASONS? OR, JUST ONE?'

Lollipop Love

Ours was a lollipop love,
Innocent and sweet,
Did we find a panel to hide
in each other's heart?
We were comfortable,
Living without a care or trouble,
Knowing that for each other
we would always be there,
Then came the ring,
An exciting thing,
But once the commitment was made,
things changed,
We began to analyze each other more critically,
Love melted like wood burning in flame,
It was not meant to be,
The Gods of fate called the shots,
They knew ours was a childlike romance,
We had not slipped into maturity,
And our feelings crumbled
like Vesuvius' showers of ash,
A long nightmarish time sprang to life,
And time moved on, as it always does,
Life was never the same,
We each lost a part of our tender hearts,
Never to be retrieved again,

But always to be remembered,
To this day, I have never matured,
But if memory serves me well,
I thoroughly enjoyed every moment of our...

Lollipop Love

A Scrap Of Paper

When I was a child I went to Parochial School,
That was many years ago,
And the nuns lived by a conservation rule
To this day, I can still see one Sister using a piece
of a used mailed envelope for scrap paper,
It was not just for fun, or a fool's caper,
It was sincere, to help save a tree,
Those of that era were thinking of the future
for you and me,
Every time I throw away an envelope,
I think about that nun,
I look around at all the waste, and ask –
What have we done?
Better still, 'What are we continuing to do?'
Too few consider waste a problem – too few,
One morning, not too long ago,
I received 35 pieces of mail,
All donation requests; I truly wanted to wail,
Most became part of my dry waste for that day,
I wanted to cry; what can I say?
I am drowning in paper;
not only regular mail, but catalogues too,
To be honest, I am never through,
And with each piece of paper I throw away, I say,
"What a waste of time, money, and effort
what a shameful display,"
And I picture that lone nun decades ago writing
on a scrap of used envelope paper,

God's conservation messenger –
making the world safer,
Saving a tree, and preventing a flood
somewhere on **Earth**,
Providing a home for some wee creatures
to live and give birth,
How callous we are, unthinking;
being ruled by want not need,
And we and future generations, will pay – pay indeed,
In everything we do, it is time to think about waste,
Stop whatever you are doing; don't act in haste,
Think about God's creation and
our responsibility to Our Maker,
Now you too can think about,
as I often do, that special nun, and

A Scrap Of Paper

Being Alone

Come to think of it,
I have been alone most of my life,
Never a sister to a sister,
never a mother, never a wife,
Strange way to live, if you ask me,
That is probably why crowds make me nervous;
somewhere else I would rather be,
I am very content most times to be alone,
Sometimes, I even hate the phone,
But, never when my friends call,
Most times that's a pleasure; I have a ball,
Being alone allows me to think;
concentrate on many things,
It is like being in a playground full of swings,
I love to write but
I find that my thought process differs from others,
Those who prefer crowds,
parties, noise, their druthers,
But my state of aloneness began
when I was very young,
It is quiet and peaceful, but I believe
it makes one a little more high-strung,
My father passed away when I was five; just a tot,
My mother went to work; I was alone a lot,
My grandmother, as I recall was sweet and caring,
But no match for my doing and daring,
My brother, five years older did his thing,
had his own friends; surprised?

But at five, I was still totally supervised,
Rightly so!
I had not developed any mojo,
Family friends chipped in and I would go
when necessary from place to place,
I think that is how I became so possessive of
'my things' – 'my space,'
At twelve, my grandmother whom I loved dearly,
passed away,
I was more or less, on my own from that day,
One of my favorite Uncles, Jack, who lived upstairs in
the same six family house, played the guitar;
he and I became very close,
Most often, he was my home away from home host,
Every neighbor and storekeeper became my guardians too,
They would ID strangers roaming the streets;
they too protected me as I grew,
I had many friends, mostly boys,
because I loved sports,
In that time, that was totally unexpected;
I played many courts,
I was super competitive as life moved on,
And I had wonderful adults to lean upon,
When I wasn't climbing fences,
I was playing in the streets,
The outdoors was a cornucopia of treats,
I did the grocery shopping and many home chores,
And spent a lot of time in local food stores,
While waiting for my mother to return home on the bus,
I would help the fruit market pack away it wares,
It was an education; I learned the good produce
from the bad, and never said, "Who cares?"
That was their life, their livelihood,
And at a very young age, I understood,
All the shopkeepers knew me well,

None would ever cheat me, or throw in a bad lemon;
or I would tell my neighbors,
They were all fair and so was I,
I learned very young, whom to trust and why,
But I was very much alone,
Until of course, my working mom would return home,
She was so busy; there was little time to share,
But bless her, the cupboard was never bare,
She had her hands full at home, while
handling a full-time job; lots to do,
She worked, and worked, and worked, until through,
There was little time for helping with school chores,
I had fish and turtles, and a small plot of dirt in the yard
to keep me company in and outdoors,
My mom planted vegetables; tilled the soil,
Fresh corn, string beans, lettuce, tomatoes,
cucumbers ~ a regular 'farmer's goil,'
It served two purposes, now that I look back,
For her, a relieving of tensions and an easing of budgetary
woes – for pinching pennies there was no lack,
I learned early in life, you must give to get,
And until I die, that lesson I will never forget,
Nobody knew, least of all me, the inner fear I possessed
about my mother giving up, running away,
Running from all the work, responsibility, heartache and
drudgery day after day,
What a living hell; what a nightmare,
That was love beyond compare,
For some reason, as young as I was,
I understood,
What the true meaning was of the word,
motherhood,
As I recall family members had a lot to say,
but rarely if ever, went out of their way,
Make her take in 'boarders;' ease the financial dent,

They became family members to help pay the rent,
Another nightmare on her plate,
They all tried to control me,
and added untold burdens; what a fate,
They were old, did nothing to help;
sat in chairs from morning to night,
Criticizing, taking not giving, telling my mom what and
how to do; I do not know how my mom did not take flight,
She was left to care for them, as they waned and became ill,
Left to take care of their 'goodbyes;'
burying them on Eternal Hill,
Families, I learned early on
can often create problems beyond belief,
To hear them, their hearts were most often in the right place,
but to me, their minds and mouths fell into 'Good Grief!'
Notice, there's little mention of my 'big brother;'
he was old enough and smart enough to flee the scene,
That is how I became so aware of nature; that was my escape...
beauty on the beam,
I used to climb out the back window, when my guardians
(renting aunts) would not let me out the apartment front door,
Oh, I did that many times, but never kept score,
I never told my mom, she had enough on her mind,
But I knew how to escape and find what I wanted to find,
I helped and loved all the stray kittens in the yard,
I always waited patiently for everything – that was hard,
I loved my summers in Huntington on Long Island, for the season,
They were great – swimming and sports every day, board games
and pinochle at night; taught me how to win/lose and reason,
Fall came quickly, and that meant back to Brooklyn for me;
back to school and the good ole reinforcement
of the "Golden Rule,"
Don't laugh; it defines **respect**
and remains life's best survival tool,
It has two Biblical references – Matt 7:12 and Luke 6:31

A little religion never hurts anyone,
Well after the initial shock of returning to a daily routine,
time set the pace,
Year-in and year-out, winter and spring did fly by;
it was quite a race,
I no longer have my Huntington pleasures,
Except for the wonderful lifelong memory treasures,
I have now matured enough to go out
and earn a "fin" or two,
No more daily beach bathing under the blue,
No more daily "Good Humor Ice Cream Truck" filled
with my favorites – the ice cream cup, Popsicle and cone,
However, I am still walking through life,
now on the downside of the hill

Being Alone

What A Wonderful Sunrise

My goodness, it is **September 11, 2001,**
Where did the summer go?
It's an ordinary day, one like any other,
The alarm rang at its precise setting,
And my tootsies hit the rug a runnin',
I only allowed an hour to take care of all my chores,
before riding to the Lake Ronkonkoma Railroad Station,
And that was a nightmare,
Everyone was trying to outdo everyone else,
No one wanted to be behind anyone,
Three lanes of speeding vehicles,
taking turns in the grabbing the first position,
Occasionally, a souped-up motorcyclist
would give you a jolt, as he revved his engine to
let you know, "Watch out, I'm here,"
I drove about five miles south on
the William Floyd, and then another
ten miles, after I connected with the
Long Island Expressway (LIE),
Once I headed west on the LIE, the sun was on the rise,
What a beautiful sight,
It "snuck" up behind me, and blinded me in the rearview mirror,
As hazardous as it was, it was gorgeous,
It was varying shades of yellow and orange, brilliant,
I cannot say that it did not distract,
and interfere with normal driving,
Most of the time you had to duck its reflection,
as you moved forward,

You blessed it's beauty, and cursed it's dangerous glare,
As it climbed the steps of heaven to its rightful rise,

I distinctly remember thinking as I approached the station,
What a beautiful day!

"What A Wonderful Sunrise"

My Torn '911' Shoes

Are they special?
Yes!

They are not pretty by any means,
They are heavy duty, black, laced *Easy Spirits*,
They are comfortable, and keep me upright,
At this point, I will add most of the time,
It is not the shoes that put them into
a class all their own,
It is the events of the day,
that put them on the memory pedestal,

The day dawned as any other,
I prepared to catch the 6:41 a.m. L.I.R.R. train,
at the Lake Ronkonkoma Station,
Yes, it was a wild commute,
I had to drive 20 miles, before I parked the car,
and put my tootsies on the platform,
On 911 however, the traffic was particularly slow,
And even though I had indoor parking,

91

none of my usual spaces was available,
I ended up on an upper level rather than street level,
Both these events were unusual,
When I hopped out of my car,
I had to walk down two flights of stairs,
I should say, run down, because I had very little time
to cross the street, and pop into the waiting train,
I was running as quickly as I could,
when suddenly without warning, I fell,
There was absolutely nothing to cause the spill,
I checked the ground after I got up, and later that evening,
My two shoes were ripped across the top,
but not enough to warrant going home,
As I tried to raise this mighty body,
a lovely young man approached to offer assistance,
What did he hear?
Much to my embarrassment, I yapped, "O, shit!"
When I looked up and saw him looking down,
I immediately apologized,
He assured me as the gentleman he was,
he would have said the same thing,
"Can you get up?"
"I think so,"
Once on my feet,
he suggested that I not go any further than home,
"I said I can't even consider that,
I've got to get to work,"
He said, "That was nasty fall,"
I said, "Do me a favor, please,"
"Sure,"
"Help me get that train,"
"Are you sure?"
"Yes,"
He grabbed me by the arm, and we both
flew across the intersection and unto the train,

Since it was my regular train,
I knew a lot of people,
My hands were bleeding, my knees were scrapped
(I couldn't figure that one out).
My slacks were dirty, but not torn),
and all I needed were some additional Band-Aids,
Everyone was saying the same thing,
"You should have gone home,"
By the time I got to the city, everything ached,
I guess my "knight in shining armor,"
and all my train buddies were right,
I should have gone home,
Guess what? When I got to the office, everyone said,
"You should have gone home,"
I followed my normal routine; I turned on
my computer, and open the first of my two cups of tea,
It was only 8:15 a.m., and most of my co-workers
were setting up their workstations,
It was a beautiful fall morning,
The sun was shining brightly;
the sky was clear with billowy white clouds,
The air was crisp,
but still held some summer warmth,
Looking out from a 12th story window
in Manhattan on such day was a treat,
Then, the world literally fell apart,
We couldn't believe what we were seeing or hearing,
A plane slammed into the World Trade Center,
We believed at first that it was an accident,
But when it was followed by
a second plane hitting the second building,
We knew, we were at war,

I remembered very clearly
how many times that morning,

I was told, "You should have gone home,"
Apparently, everyone knew better than I,
One tower fell, I cried
as I watched it pancake upon itself,
And not too long after that
the second tower was gone,
Black smoke wrote history
on a beautiful, clear, blue sky,
Yes, there was fear, but no outright panic,
Plans developed instantaneously,
As reports came in, actions were taken,
Originally, we were not to leave our building,
Within two minutes of that decision,
We were told to go,
Should we take the elevator?
No! Yes! No!
Since I couldn't walk the stairs, I had no choice,
They announce, "This will be the last elevator,"
I got on, and prayed,
When we stepped out into the street,
No one knew what to do,
Everyone was looking into the sky,
Emergency equipment was flying by,
The only noise in the city from that point on was
sirens,
But millions of New Yorkers behaved
as only New Yorkers do in times of extreme emergency,
Everyone shared everything they had to help each other,
Stores were closed or closing,
Cell phones were at a premium, as was food and water,
The roadbeds were left open for ambulances,
police cars, fire engines, and those who were "in-charge,"
Strange as it may seem,
millions of people controlled themselves,
When one sidewalk was filled to capacity,

The crowds filled the next,
But no one stepped into the roadbed,
America flags popped out of nowhere,
They were in store windows,
On buildings,
On the train,

Where did they come from?

Americans were instantaneously united,
United however in silence,
Have you ever been in a crowd of millions,
and not heard a sound?
It is quite an eerie experience,
You almost were afraid to speak, and
break that oppressive silence and sorrow,
Yet somehow,
we each figured out for ourselves what to do,
Some headed downtown to start their trek
across the Brooklyn Bridge,
Others headed North...
Some florists and shopkeepers handed people
roses and flowers,
Many were looking to buy sneakers
before they walked miles to their homes,
And where was I? I was walking with a co-worker,
her first day back to work after shoulder surgery,
The two of us, walking wounded,
headed to Penn Station,
We were told that there were no trains running
and that the Station was closed,
We were also informed that there were
no hotel rooms available in the City,
I wonder why,
We had no choice but to

take our chances at Penn Station,
So, on we went,
When we reached our destination,
people were absolutely wonderful,
They noted our disabilities and without question
helped us to the front of the line,
They put us right in front of the staircase
leading to the trains,
It was true that no trains were running,
They were inspecting the railroad tracks,
So, we waited for hours,
The police were all around and controlled
a very well behaved crowd,
We knew that when we were permitted to go down to
the platform to board a train there would be a stampede,
My co-worker and I were apprehensive,
I couldn't walk too well and wondered
how I would manage the stairs,
Two people literally picked me up by my elbows
and carried me to the train,
And, they made sure that I got a seat,
However in the confusion, we all were separated –
I never saw them again,
I do not know who they were;
but I hope they were blessed for their lifetimes,
Everyone, particularly those covered in the
World Trade Center dust,
were desperately seeking water – to no avail,
To add a little levity to this moment, besides my purse,
I grabbed my insulated lunch bag, when I left the office,
Who else would think about food
in a moment like that except me?
I shared,
I had a large bunch of juicy grapes…
Everyone was delighted,

It wasn't much, but it helped,
When we left the Station, our railroad car was
half empty; we didn't understand
why, given the crowds waiting to board,
We were totally enlightened when
we reached the Jamaica Station,
Thousands of people were waiting to hop on,
Too many to fill our car,
which was now breathing room only,
Each stop was a nightmare,
People had to get off to let others disembark,
and then get back on,
We were all starving for news,
One man, sitting to the right of me had a small hand-held
TV, which he was desperately trying to get to work,
Finally, some bright light gave him some
aluminum foil to wrap around the antenna,
Voilà, the picture and sound came;
not clear, but 'good' enough,
Then he had to get off,
Everyone was everyone's friend,
It was as though we were family,
In a way, I guess we were,
I met some wonderful folks,
I would be totally remiss, if I did not
mention one young lady, who helped me,
She was a Spanish radio reporter;
I wish I could remember her name,
But should she read this,
I hope she knows how I blessed her,
In between observing the passengers
and eaves-dropping, I would look out the window,
The smoke was still rising,
carrying new souls to Heaven,
And everywhere I looked, there were

American flags,
Even on the backs of homes and garages,
I do not remember how long
that trip was, but it was long,
By the time I disembarked
I was feeling the effects of the day,
I just wanted to get in my car and head home,
As I approached my driveway,
I saw my neighbors waiting,
They didn't even give me a moment
to compose myself,
I guess I was rude;
I didn't even roll down my window,
I pointed that I was going into the garage,
and rolled forward,
I closed the door, as I looked down at my torn
911 shoes,
I thanked God and wept.

And with all that going on around me,
one of the things I remembered the most was,

My Torn '911' Shoes

9/11/2001

I reviewed with sorrow the events of the day,
Even though they were very far away,
So many years, and the memory lingers on,
I can still see the smoke; the buildings were gone,
The sky throughout was clear and blue,
But the chill of the loss, cut through and through,
And as my train traveled further and further away,
my heart was solemn, on display,
It was showing its hurt, distress and dismay,
Only murmurs of conversations could be heard,
The shock was obvious; it silenced every bird,
Flags were flying where they never did before,
They fluttered on every home
and business – window, wall and door,
An inexplicable historical moment never to be forgot,
Americans joined forces – tempers were 'hot,'
Once again, we were a Nation; we were one,
Ready to do battle; ready to overcome,
Everyone was helping everyone else to cope,
Consoling, strengthening and offering hope,
Nerves were frayed;
there was without a doubt, some fear,
Most in my train car had confirmed the whereabouts
of those they held dear,
Only a few were unaware of their loved ones,
or waiting for news, location corrections,
Concern and encouragement were offered with the
most positive projections,

Some in the group were still covered
with the towers' dust,
Shaking from what they had seen, and
wondering how they would adjust,
Everyone on that day knew everyone else;
we were suddenly, instant friends,
The next day was eerie;
we all agreed, we were still in shock,
obviously no one comprehended,
Many of my regular commuters were nowhere
to be seen; there was many an empty seat,
I prayed for them, that they survived and
were simply from yesterday's events –"beat"
As I walked through Penn Station with thousands of
fellow-commuters, everything had changed,
Shops were closed, there was no sound;
daily routines had been rearranged,
Soldiers with rifles were
on guard; each in a strategical place,
Everyone was herded along at a rapid pace,
Policemen were guarding escalators,
and points of egress,
Everyone was feeling the air of distress,
Thousands of commuters, but not a sound was heard,
No frivolity, no laughter, not a single word,
I remember thanking a patrolman on guard,
But there was no response; that was so strange, so odd,
Even the streets were eerily quiet –
not even a honking horn,
It was an instant change from morn to morn,
There was a strange odor permeating the air,
But no one would say what it was; they wouldn't dare,
We all knew; death has an odor all its own,
Amazing how we all on our own had instantly grown,
And too I note, how suddenly we all had become

quite suspicious, uneasy,
As I walked deep in thought, I was very alert and
somewhat queasy,
I felt so alone and thought how scary, how weird,
There were people all around,
on all sides; was that what I feared?
In fact, a tall, young man stepped up right beside me,
Could he tell what I was feeling; what did he see?
He looked down, smiled and said,
"Hello, happy for the company?"
But that greeting did not come without
my questions, which were many,
He was carrying two steel boxes –
one long and narrow, the other square, both heavy,
I have a question, but do I dare?
Yes! I looked him in the eye and
said, "Is that your lunchware?"
He laughed and replied "This one is (the smaller box),
he rattled the other, it made a metallic noise,
I laughed and said, "Are they your toys?"
"No, I am in construction, these are my tools,"
I felt as though I was sailing on a "ship of fools,"
Here we were back to our routines,
not twenty-four hours after going to war,
Not knowing what was the score,
We walked, and talked, and
I think we enjoyed that time, the chat,
But all too soon, he said,
"I work up that way, so I will scat"
I still had three of four street blocks to go,
All the regular fruit stands were no show,
I felt quite relieved when I walked into my building,
with all the new security in place,
I was happy to show my employee Id
and see a familiar face,

Our lives had been uprooted in an instant;
no doubt about that,
And now we have a new way to live,
a new life, a new perilous habitat,
Today is September Twelfth,
Two Thousand and One,
Yesterday, another
Day of Infamy,

9/11/2001

Yesterday's Sundays

Ah! Sunday,
A day of rest – for some,
A day for worship – for some,
A day set aside to change one's routine –
for some,
But, today's Sunday is no longer
the day it was in times gone by,
In times when the Church bells pealed
and families joined together in pew and prayer,
When people listened and obeyed the "Father's" of Faith,
It truly was a day of change,
There was something different about the morning,
The smell of fresh perked coffee and bacon
wafted into every crevice in the house,
The sun even seemed to rise in a different manner,
That was because we all slept later, and
the battle for the bathroom hadn't begun,
Newspapers and slippers and pajamas pervaded the scene,
The biggest decision of that moment was, who got
the funnies, the sports pages, or the "real news" first,
There was always momentary commotion,
until everyone got something to read,
Ah! A return to the serene scene,
For all, it was a day to change the mindset and demeanor,
Specially prepared dinners were served to mark the day,
No work, no school, no scheduled moments of play,
It was a day to catch one's breath,
To smell the roses and fresh air,

and watch the birds take flight,
To enjoy and capture the horizon's
moments of sunrise and sunset,
Take a moment or two to pen a nice newsy letter,
As the aroma of the repast to come, filled the home,
Company was common and most welcomed,
Conversation never lacked,
There were no telephones, cell phones or computers,
opened stores for shopping,
Sandy beach visits – Lemon aide and paper fans for summer,
Hot chocolate and drafty living rooms for cooler days,
The warmth of those special moments always lingered,
The glint in an eye, when surprised,
The broadness of a smile, when pleased,
And of course, the hugs to be remembered with thanks,
and love to last a lifetime,
Then slowly, as the day waned,
Routines returned,
and preparations began for the week ahead,
As the dawn of the new day broke forth,
everyone knew what they had to do,
On the home-front, leftovers where set for dinner,
the wash was hand done and hung; the house was emptied
and ready for Mom's cleaning and clearing,
The routine was set and lived,
And now, only the memories remain of the days gone by,
Including, of course,

Yesterday's Sundays

Times Change

I loved the streets of Brooklyn,
Particularly the first one on which I lived,
It was "home,"
Who needed more?
It was filled with family,
good neighbors and friends,
It danced with games and fun,
It was alive,
It was safe,
Everyone knew everyone,
Who should be there and who should not,
Windows were left open day and night
to cool each room,
There was plenty of cross-ventilation,
Sometimes however, it "cooled" with hotter air
than it already held,
There was little to no fear of anyone
who did not belong coming in,
We could all sleep in peace,
Hot was hot and there was no escape,
Well, perhaps a small oscillating fan,
No air conditioning then,
We all prayed for rain in beastly weather
just for some cool air,
It would wash the streets too, as it brought relief,
In summer, I always prayed for fall (still do),
Not only for cool air, but the start of school,
I loved school,

I wasn't a very good student; quite dumb,
Funny thing, I respected summer,
For like any child I had more time to play,
And it was Daylight Savings Time; longer light,
I could go to the public pool twice a day –
once for free,
I could hang out in the park,
swing on the swings and climb trees,
I could play handball, baseball,
roller skate, do anything I wanted to do,
And so I did,
Who ever questioned the heat of summer?
It was summer; we knew what to expect,
Everyone enjoyed a good movie and
the theaters were cool,
So were the cellars, even though dangerous,
Who knew who lurked in the dark corners
and storage bins?
Even on the hottest day, I never walked anywhere,
I ran,
I'd jump every cellar door I could find,
I did not want to stop,
For when I did, the cooling breeze
was nowhere to be found,
The 2 cent slice of watermelon right off
a cake of ice was grand,
And so was the stolen chunk of ice,
snipped from the back of the ice truck,
It was filthy…full of germs, and very refreshing,
The driver would always chase us,
but not with much enthusiasm,
We only took the small pieces that would melt
before the truck reached the top of the hill,
It was a time when milk and cream were in one bottle;
that and juice were delivered to your door step,

or placed on your window sill,
Bakery goods – cupcakes, bread, and sweet treats
were purchase from delivery trucks,
And they were the "real thing" –
not, 80% chemicals – no the "real thing,"
Fresh fruit came on horse-drawn carts,
A whole cantaloupe was 5 cents,
and the fruit man would slice it
so you could sit on the stoop and eat it fresh right there,
I can still taste that fruit – filled with DDT
and other fertilizer that are forbidden today,
Hmm, hmm good,
Funny, we survived,
We survived with fewer ailments than exist today,
I loved buying a "gill" of my favorite ice cream,
How many today, know what a "gill" is?
Check it out,
Or, a mellow roll – Wow! What?
Candy was candy then too… it will never be the same,
It was not individually wrapped,
That takes away loads of flavor,
An Italian Cream was only one cent, and when the
owner felt generous, he would give you two for a penny,
They were bite-sized, and delicious,
There was nothing better than a "Hooton Bar,"
Milk chocolate, goober nuts and raisins to die for,
And who could forget the
Double Bubble and Bazooka chewing gum?
It not only pulled out your fillings, but your teeth,
I would probably have more of my own today
without that pink, bubble producing treat,
But summer faded fast, and along came fall,
The leaves would rustle up and down the street,
as they chased each other,
Time for school and homework and early dark,

Darkness came right on time, to call the end of summer,
Curtains were drawn early,
It was time for readin', writin' and 'rithmatic,
And now, what do we have?
Memories …

Times Change

Huntington, NY Stories
To Warm The Heart

"Summer Memories to Cherish"
I won't let go,
No…
These are my memories which will live forever,
At least as long as I do,

Walking down Huntington Bay Hills Road to meet
Marie and Stanley, as they returned home from work,
Time was falling into dusk, and the cool
evening air was always welcomed,
I would always pick the flowers on the side of the road
to give to them as I hopped into their car,
I was always happy to see
my host and hostess return home,
They were tired I was sure, but never let me know it,
Dinner was waiting, as was their son,
who was younger than I,
Given that, he was not permitted to walk
with me to greet them,
He remained at home with Grandma,
I enjoyed that time as much as
my morning walks on the beach,
For a "City Girl," this was Heaven,
Just the sound of the crickets,
and lovely lightening bugs all around,

No traffic, loud horns, and
screaming kids running wild,
Of course, when I went home,
I would be one of them too,
But I would be tanned, and healthy,
and ready for the next term's challenge,
I wonder if I ever let *Marie and Stanley* know
how grateful I was for their hospitality, their love,
I doubt it,
After all, I was very young,
But maybe they will somehow hear it now,
I used to love playing cards with *Grandma Jordan*,
every late night,
After my little playmate fell asleep,
I would sneak into *Mrs. Jordan's* bedroom and we would
play pinochle as long as we could,
When the family car would arrive, I would have to disappear,
Up to the attic,
Hot as God's fiery acres,
I would think about what I would do the following day,
The yard, the beach, getting drenched by the garden hose,
How about badminton, and horseshoes, and croquet,
And all of that would be before two visits and
swimming at the private Club House beach,
I was spoiled and pampered for two few summers,
One summer my host and hostess bought me a
tennis racket, which I still have,
And they paid for me to have
private tennis lessons, Wow!
One of my favorite memories was
hitting the tennis ball for the first time,
It went over the net neatly, and kept going on a fly
into the far neighbor's backyard,
It went so far that no one would retrieve it,

Then I learned, and fell in love with that sport,
Fishing was great too,
They had a small motor boat, and a dinghy,
At that time, I even baited my own hook,
But as I grew older, somehow I got out of that practice,
Those hours always passed too quickly,
While others dawdled,
The mail and the Good Humor Ice Cream Truck
took forever to show,
I missed Brooklyn and my mom, of course,
That's why I fervently waited for the mail,
There was always money for ice cream,
And every now and again,
the mail truck would show up with games from home,
My mom never forgot to surprise us with new games
to perk up the dead of summer,
Speaking of my mom,
she was very thoughtful and very special,
Except on one occasion,
Her sister, my aunt, made a fateful decision,
and my mom agreed,
It happened the day that my aunt drove
my mom to pick me up,
It was the end of the summer,
and I had to go back to Brooklyn,
I had worked so hard all summer to strengthen
my swimming and diving,
I practiced endlessly for the competition,
which was held on the last day,
The end of the season,
I had a very faded and worn two piece bathing suit,
It was quite grungy,
but would serve it purpose beautifully,
It was light and gave me more speed in the water,

111

Well, my aunt decided it looked awful and
I should wear her beautiful white one-piece latex suit,
And with my tan, I would look so much better,
So, they sewed and tucked and made the suit fit me,
I hated it,
But, being the age that I was, I had no say,
I lost all the races, except one,
I took third place in one diving event,
Even that surprised me,
For when I hit the water, I also hit the bottom,
The suit was so heavy it took me straight down,
I scraped my legs on the bottom,
I had a hard time finding daylight,
I guess I have never forgiven anyone
for that debacle,
I cried all the way home,
There were no words of consolation,
None,
Nor would there be even today,
Case closed.
But there was a much better story
to come out of my swimming days,
I joined up to become a Junior Life Guard,
Let's put that into perspective,
I was from Brooklyn,
All the other participants were local,
They knew each other,
went to the same school and churches,
attended the same socials,
And then, there was me,
It was a difficult course,
and the final exam for Certification was
really grueling for me,
But, I was determined,

112

On that final day,
we all had to report to a certain area on the beach,
One-by-one, we had to perform certain tasks,
including an actual Fireman's carry rescue,
Then there were others
where we were all in the water together,
We also demonstrated a human chain rescue,
But the final task was swimming for an
extremely long period of time without stopping,
while demonstrating all the strokes
we needed to survive,
I believe there were eight or ten
who were seeking Certification,
I never really felt part of the group,
because I was not really part of that community,
Everyone was helpful and pleasant,
but a little standoffish,
I was probably the weakest of the group,
And, I did not feel as though I would
survive that final testing,
I was the last one in the water struggling
to complete each of the required strokes,
The instructor was ready to call it quits for me,
when the entire group began to shout,
"You can do it, keep going, don't stop – keep going,"
And so I did,
Thanks to each of them, I was Certified,
I became a Junior Life Guard ...
And Thank God, I never had to save anyone.
More memories...
Wednesday night at the beach was movie night,
We never missed movie night,
Everyone got a punk, and it had to be lit,
Keep those bugs away!

It was a typical children's event,
Movie or not, there was talking,
and laughing, and squealing, and treats,
I do not remember one of the movies, not one,
But, I remember not missing a "Night at the Movies,"

"Huntington, NY Stories To Warm The Heart"

'Summer Memories to Cherish'

Huntington, NY

My Forever Life – My Forever Memory

———————❧❧❧———————

I was but a child,
Yet, I felt the beauty of God's Earth all around,
I heard the rolling tide,
buzzin' bees and caroling birds,
as I walked the roadways and beaches,
I never missed a passing cloud,
I experienced nature, turbulent or calm,
And, it was mine to enjoy,
The wind could be a whisper,
or a howling, whistling terror,
It could be more powerful than man's electricity,
transformers and wires,
Dawn and me, alone together
I loved to go to the shore and walk along the beach,
without fear, in the early morning hours,
I wondered if the turf rested at night,
before it welcomed me each day,
How beautiful, its quiet rolling beat,
In calm, it was barely audible,
But to me it was a quiet melody of joy,
A rhythm of life,
As young as I was,
I was aware of who I was - my being…my freedom,
The only break in those cherished moments of peace
was an occasional sea gull checking me out,
Who could have asked for more?
The swell of the Bay,

the wild honeysuckle and roses sharing their fragrances,
The morning drone of the cicadas now falling into sleep,
O, how I wanted to believe and say with certainty,
"this is all there is to life,"
It was quite the glory,
But I knew even then, it was simply a snippet of reality,
A memory to store and recall in some tomorrow time,
Just a few summers – ever so brief –
too few short visits to a Heavenly place called…

Huntington, NY
My Forever Life – My Forever Memory

Anything For Thanksgiving?

Oh, the things I remember, about certain yesterday times
when I was young and 'so wise,'
My mom definitely did not want me to
ring door bells and beg,
That's what she felt about begging on Thanksgiving Day,
That was the only time I did that,
Not on Halloween,
But I would grab a shopping bag, hide it under my coat,
before I went out to play on Thanksgiving Day,
I wanted to do what all the other kids did,
Most times we would go in a group,
But sometimes, I would go on my own,
That was best,
It certainly wasn't safe,
I never gave that a thought,
I did pretty good too,
I came home and shared the fruit and nuts,
coins, cookies, etc.
No candy…that was mine,
What could be wrong?
My mom would reprimand me, of course,
when I brought the bag home,
However, she was so busy with dinner,
the upset would quickly fade,
In fact, it didn't come back until the next year
when I was old enough to truly understand,
she shared her objections with me,
She was embarrassed to know that I had begged,

She was nervous because I was going
into six family houses,
Anybody could be hiding in the halls,
She didn't want the neighbors to think she didn't feed me,
Final statement – "Please don't beg,"
By the time my mom shared that with me,
I was too old to beg,
But I have never forgotten those days,

Anything For Thanksgiving?

I found out much later, it's a Brooklyn thing

My 50¢ Christmas Tree

In 1955 we moved, and did not have room for a
Christmas tree in our new apartment,
I was devastated, and my mom knew it,
So, being the magnanimous person she was,
she said, "If you can figure something out, do it,
But, I will not give you the money to buy a tree,"
We had a stand, lights, ornaments,
That's all we needed, except the space to set it up,
I got angry and said, "I'll find a tree,"
I think it was late on Christmas Eve,
So, I walked and walked
and questions some neighbors,
"Where might I buy a Christmas Tree?
Go this way and that, and you'll find the lot,
No problem,
Good, one problem solved,
Next…money,
I only had fifty-cents,
Full trees, what were left, were selling for one
to two and one-half dollars,
It was a bitter cold night and the man wanted to
shut down the business,
He wanted to go home,
I couldn't blame him, so I looked around,
Slim pickin's, but I found just what I wanted,
I bargained, and he sold me a tree for fifty-cents,
It was a perfect size and it would just fit in the
corner next to the window on the left,

He tied the tree and put a handle on it for me,
I had a long walk home, and by then, it was dark,
and oh so cold,
Of course, it wasn't his best tree,
They had long since been sold,
But, it was fine for me for fifty-cents,
It was only about four feet high, and heavy,
I schlepped it home, through the lobby, onto
the elevator and into our apartment,
Talk about determination,
Well, God love her, my mom helped me to untie the
beauty,
And as I walked to find the stand, she yelled,
"You 'gotta' take this back,
that man cheated you."
Of course, I objected vehemently,
Besides the place was closed for Christmas,
"What kind of tree is this?
There's no back"
So, I smiled and said, "Yeah, I know,
It's half a tree, so we can set it up against the wall,
That's why I bought it.
It is a perfect fit for the space we have,
It will be beautiful,"
And so it was,
It cost every penny I had, but it was well worth it,

My 50¢ Christmas Tree

'Cheese It!' The Cops

When I was very young – just a kid,
I imitated others; I did just what they did,
I would watch older men flip coins
against buildings on the block,
And the winner would pick up all
the coins, with a loud, "It's a lock!"
It was a game – fun to watch,
Some players were great, top-notch,
What did I know; we were 'look-outs' for
those guys; it was gambling, not hop-scotch,
For when we would see the police car coming up
the hill, we would yell… 'Cheese It, the Cops,'
The men would scatter, be on the run,
We thought that was really great fun,
Besides, we'd get the coins they left behind,
The older kids got the big coins,
and we would keep whatever we could find,
I don't remember ever thinking it was wrong,
I just wanted to be one of the 'gang' – belong,
But when the day came that I found out the truth,
That ended that fun in my youth,
But I can still hear the cry, loud and clear;
everyone pulled out the stops,
The men took it on the 'lamb,'
when they heard us yell …

'Cheese It!' The Cops

121

It Is So Obvious When You Are Oblivious To Your Own State Of Oblivion

It definitely has something to do with forgetting,
No, maybe it's simply a state of indifference,
With a title like this, it's surely forgetfulness,
Oh, what's the difference?
Whatever it is, it's obvious,
But, to whom?
Certainly not me,
And, another thing,
Who knows what I forgot, if I can't remember?
And that's obvious too,
Particularly, when you look down,
and you are wearing only one shoe,
My, my, what can one do?
For starters, put on the other shoe, before you forget,
You know, before you remember, not to forget,
Or, forget not to remember,
Where am I now?
I'm totally lost,
Could it be simply, that ...

It Is So Obvious When You Are Oblivious To Your Own State Of Oblivion

Snowflakes

There is no silence as deep as that following
a fresh fallen snow,
It's a silence that beckons sound,
The winds howling would have ceased,
Too tired, no doubt, to continue on,
The birds, if lucky, would still be nestling close,
Worn from battling "Mother Nature's" fury,
We look out from within, with rapture,
For the gift of beauty that
has been laid out before us,
Whether in sunlight, or lamplight,
snowflakes will always be found chattering,
With reflective rainbow messages,
Diamonds each,
So just step back, and enjoy their silent notes;
enjoy their rare, silent sight-tones,
Those only transmitted by new born

Snowflakes

TODAY

Today is today. Profound, profound. The living moment.

Speak to me time...tick, tock, tick tock. Your rhythm is leading the way diminuendos/accelerando. You are in control. I know you are not only living for yourself, but for me, for everyone. Yeah, but I also know you are living your agenda too.

You, my readers, just journeyed with me through my Yesterday." It ended with a poem entitled "Snowflakes." Silent, colorless glistening life. Oh, if only ours could be so pure and beautiful.

All our "Yesterdays" no matter how lived open the flood gates and lead us into our living

"Today..."

A Silent, Visual Dichotomy

'The Cumulus Congestus'

Magnificent!
Dark gray, silver Cumulus Congestus clouds,
They floated,
They gathered,
They puffed,
They changed color,
Deep silver blue to shiny silver white,
They looked as though they were very angry;
getting ready to fight,
They billowed upward
and stretched sideward as well,
They appeared as though
they did not know which way to go,
Maybe their indecision caused distress,
Normally such gatherings roll with thunder,
Produce wind and rain, and snow,
But strangely, they spoke not a word,
Just created…

A Silent, Visual Dichotomy

Dry Drowning

Not in an ocean or lake or body of blue,
No, drowning in endless,
repetitive conversations of old, not new,
Drowning in paper work that
continues to pile high,
After given constant attention;
it causes one to give up and sigh,
But I do not intend to drown unnaturally-dry,
and make history,
Although it might lead to quite a mystery,
Lungs filled with water, trapped by paper dust,
Someone will figure that out I trust,
Bring on some super sleuths, diggers deep,
Until 'case resolved;' they will have no sleep,
But,can they help me out of a telephone trap?
People who never stop talking,
holding a talk-a-thon on an endless track?
They find some pleasure in filling
their empty moments with chatter,
The day is long and using time anyway,
does not matter,
And lately I find, I am doing the same,
When someone calls who had something
worthwhile to say, their time I claim,
Living alone without a schedule,
wallowing in time,
Not being able to do what you want,
that is a blasted crime,

And to look at all the things that await being done
can drive you up a wall, or further;
footprints on the ceiling, anyone?
Then the phone rings –
'I must get 'caller ID' for self-protection,
But I would not want to hurt anyone's
feelings by rejection,
So I listen and to lighten the moment,
I participate in some verbal clowning,
While feeling trapped; while drowning, drowning...

Dry Drowning

Shred

That's all I do lately is shred, shred, shred,
And as I work and read,
I see nothing, but red, red, red,
I am the fool, no one else,
I collected this paper myself,
The computer was supposed to
eliminate it, and clutter,
Not so, say I, as I struggle and mutter,
I have seven years of saving this
picture, story and quip,
Now, I am re-reading and starting to strip,
I cannot walk, or move,
without knocking over a pile,
The expletives that result,
will leave when I arrive in my heavenly exile,
I cannot believe that I created such a mess,
And still want to save it for my writing no less,
What a pinhead; no, a jerk,
My mind should hold the answers for my work,
There are reference places all around,
The library for one, and the computer,
where endless answers can be found,
But for now, I am bound determined to succeed,
To continue to weed and weed, and weed,
My garden of paper is on its way out; it is dead,
And I will have a Machiavellian smile
to accompany each thing I

Shred

129

My Peace, Perfect Peace

Peace - that place of silence and calm,
A quiet heavenly balm,
A state in which to wash away troubles and fears,
To dry before they fall, inner tears,
Peace of mind can strengthen, overshadow, and
overcome feelings of weakness within,
Finding that level of satisfaction is finding
the freedom in one's birth origin,
A clean slate for each day's start,
For what has been said and done is gone;
only keep the good in heart,
Without the will to remove the unwanted,
peace cannot find a home,
Can you rest easy in your past days ways,
and let them roam?
If so, you always will find rest and comfort;
time to let go - release,
For then, there will be a place within for

My Peace, Perfect Peace

A Special Blend

Today, I heard a bird sing,
I looked as it flew away, as it took wing,
The sound was so pure and sweet,
I felt blessed by a special treat,
I watched as in seconds,
it reached heights untold,
No fear, no question, so tiny, so bold,
I prayed, come back, sing some more,
I won't stray too far from my door,
If it were spring, or summer,
I would open my windows too,
Just to hear you again,
get a glimpse of you,
Can spring be far behind?
Not with these thoughts in mind,
You are all seasons rolled into one;
come anytime my feathered friend,
For without a doubt, you are...

A Special Blend

131

Please, Keep It To Yourself

There is a very strange phenomenon in life;
It is a truism to be sure,
It is called a secret,
The best way to keep a secret, secret,
is to keep it to yourself,
Whether it be a secret of your own making,
or one, belonging to another,
It will not remain secret if you blabber, will it?
That is why, when one says,
"Can you keep a secret?"
I love to reply, 'Yes, but I would rather not,'
To say, 'Yes,' would be right at that moment,
and quite true,
But, how many secrets have slipped
off a loose tongue?
In most cases, the act
is totally unintentional, to be sure,
But when secrets are passed along,
just to 'stir the pot,'
The word 'deliberate' immediately
comes to mind,
That would flaw my character;
besmirch my reputation,
Secrets are best kept secret,
to keep them out of harm's way,
Parents beware; do not share
a family secret with each other,
Especially not with the young,

Definitely not with a threat of death
for any revelation,
Why place skeletons in their
mind's closet forever?
Confidence and faith can be built
in so many other ways,
For many a secret paves the way
to juicy gossip,
Often a simple secret is revealed in weakness,
Or, to release it from the teller's own closet,
Once told, it then leads to nothing less than worry,
So why reveal one problem and create another?
I guess I'm not into 'secrets' – not even one,
So –

Please, Keep It To Yourself

My Old Bone Tones

Snappin', creakin' bones,
Sing out in non-lubricated tones,
"Apply a little goose grease, if you please,
Before me bloody joints rot, or freeze,'
Now, how does one do that, I must inquire?
I sound like the 'Tin Man'
with a need so dire,
I try to keep movin' so
things stay loose, don't stick,
Staying young would really do the trick,
But, since I cannot rejuvenate
my parts – my bones,
I'll just keep on singin' loud and drown out…

My Old Bone Tones

Trust

How transparent is transparent?
Are we telling all the countries of the world,
they can get rid of their spies?
Will we be giving blueprints for how we
will operate, what we hope to use,
and for each plan of action we devise?
That concept alone defines the ground
upon which each candidate stands,
There is another "T" word that transcends
transparent; it's lost now,
somewhere in America's wastelands,
Buried in a political subterranean deep,
it is nowhere to be found; it is not a must,
It is a far more understandable and an acceptable word –
it is called...

Trust

A Changing World

What if all inanimate things suddenly
developed minds and motions of their own?

Clocks refused to tick,
Planes refused to fly,
Guns refused to fire,
Street lights decided only to work an
eight-hour night,
Pencils rebelled; refused to write and erase,
Doors worked only at will – theirs,
Computers decided
which items were to be addressed and when,
All modes of transportation (including your cars)
joined together to stop after twelve hours
and worked only a four hour week,
Eyeglasses decided only to be
worn at certain times during a day,
Faucets sprayed those who treated them roughly,
Water decided to flow only
when it felt like it, and where,
That would be a jolly, 'Johnny,' mess,
Drawers refused to open and close,
All clothes went on parade
or refused to be buttoned, snapped, or zipped,
All vegetation, meats and poultry decided
we were their food,
Can you picture your chairs, which face nothing
but endless assholes daily, walking out the door?

Garbage trucks dumping loads,
and snow plows refusing to plow,
Maybe,
I should change my title to 'Chaos,' instead of,

A Changing World

You, My Winter's Wind Went Wild

Oh, winter, oh, winter, oh, do take a rest,
You whipped wild overnight;
you went berserk, I will attest,
I felt so sorry for all the trees,
taking such a beating,
While you whipped around,
laughing and fleeting,
You were uncontrollable to say the least,
You should be ashamed of yourself, you beast,
Why not say 'goodbye,' in a more gentle way –
with a little peep?
Be happy to move out,
and take your well-deserved sleep,
I love your season,
but not when you become a child,
I have to agree with those who protest,
for I know, without a doubt...

You, My Winter's Wind Went Wild

News

I have listened for months about
which candidate to choose,
Commentators, Talk Show Hosts, are all analysts;
the hell with straight news,
Who cares what the entertainment media folks say?
Let them vote the way they want; vote their own way,
Millions of ordinary citizens make up their own minds,
Vote without commentary, as each Primary unwinds,
I don't want people to try to influence my vote,
Change my mind;
let the candidates, their platforms float,
Mass media, the daily 'upchuck'
of events, turns me off,
I am not interested in your points of view; buzz-off,
I need not be directed by union leaders, or others,
Or, be led by other party affiliations –
sisters, or brothers,
Forget it; I have a mind of my own,
I do not wish to be a political clone,
I will not be impressed by good looks and oratory,
Just give me the facts of your campaign –
no ghost story,
For a change, tell me more than just
'the what;' I need to know 'the how,'
How will you accomplish what you promise? –
tell me now,

I will make my own decision;
without a ring in my nose, I will choose,
And, please, stop the overwhelming
avalanche of analytical

News

Remember All Of This

Simple things grow harder,
as we move towards the great beyond,
The thought process slows,
memories fail to gel and bond,
One of the most challenging events, occurs
when joints take on a mind of their own,
You reach out; they deny the motion;
your goal is blown,
Better still when you handle a cup of water,
it gives whiplash in motion,
It is like having your arm
dashed upon the shore by an angry ocean,
You want to what? Run?
Walking becomes safer, sometimes even fun,
Your options diminish with each passing day,
You either resist or take the body's way,
To resist is futile; you will fail, accept
the ruler of your action – bail,
Scrub the floor on your knees?
"Where have you been – oh, please,"
Sometimes you'll get down without any trouble,
But getting up – well, I hate to burst your bubble,
Picking up things that are heavy is another test,
Will against will, at best,
So to the young I say, with hope; catch my words,
do not let them go amiss,
Listen to me, and do not be surprised; just try, yes, try to …

Remember All Of This

Oh, Flum Bum

There is no such phrase as 'Flum Bum!'
Oh, yes there is; I coined that phrase by gum,
It is one I use instead of Scarlett O'Hara's,
'O, fiddly dee, dee'
It has the same connotation to me,
I use it to express my exasperation on a good day,
Control my temper and nasty expletives,
when I am in a bad way,
It works for me, when I remember to use it,
And there is another I use
when I forget – 'Oh, flit!'
In most annoying situations
I do not get depressed and glum,
I simply call upon my 'antidotum,'

Oh, Flum Bum

Music And Me

Music is within; it freely flows,
It travels from my head to my toes,
It never leaves me – day or night,
It's a neon sign, pulsing with starlight,
It excites; it brings total pleasure,
But it must be the type I love –
the type I treasure,
And that of course depends upon
my mood and need,
Albeit melodic, soothing and slow,
or with a beat, full of speed,
And so it journeys to engulf my very being,
I can feel it, and see it without seeing,
Like the sound of a whispering reed,
or a breeze in a tree,
Always and totally engaged – just my

Music And Me

My Dream

Let my mind wander far beyond my turf,
Wander into galaxies far beyond earth,
Let me revel in the wonders of the starlit world,
Not to stay, just to visit tomorrow's world unfurled,
Like unwrapping a surprise present,
Visit the North Star, Orion, The Milky Way,
the Moon in its crescent,
Let me sense without fear,
the darkness all around – stark and deep,
And come to know that depth while I sleep,
And then return to earth by
sliding down a moon beam,
Awake refreshed, having lived…

My Dream

I Apologize

I hope I do not make people cringe,
when I call,
Organ recitals and poetry
can make some walk up a wall,
For all those I have treated so,
I apologize deeply,
And 'thank God' I only called you weekly,
Go ahead say it, but don't get too wise,
For I love you for your patience, and

I Apologize

That's A Must

I am naïve,
That, I do believe,
But, better than I was years ago,
For now I have learned, have come to know,
Many things, many ways about human kind,
They can set you a-reelin' or put you in a bind,
They can wrap you up and spit you out,
After they have used you; wear you down no doubt,
Unfortunately,
you cannot believe everything you see or hear,
And watch out when they call you, 'my dear,'
Frightening thoughts wouldn't you say?
Think it over, whatever is thrown your way,
Become sophisticated;
learn who you can trust,
In life,

That's A Must

I'm Special–This, I Know

I am a squirrel, but I am quite different –
that's known,
I was born with a swivel tail;
it stayed that way even full-grown,
I endured much laughter, as a baby and as a child,
It was an errant gene, a permanent situation;
even loved ones smiled,
But as I grew and others stopped to point at me, I was
very unhappy; for they were laughing you see,
Then I matured and faced my plight,
And found that I could bring laughter by
flicking my tail – my individual birthright,
Children loved to see my tail
facing east, when I ran west,
They were overjoyed; that sight was one of the best,
They were struck in awe,
when I simply swiveled my tail,
"What kind of squirrel is that?"
I'd reply, "Special," for I have a tall, tail tale,
They would smile, now;
I was one of the wonders of their world,
No other squirrel had a tail like mine to be unfurled,
So be happy, you never know
when things will turn around,
I changed; I learned, an answer I found,
Learn to be more precious,
because you are who you are,
Not one like all the rest, but different by far,

However, it will be up to you,
Just be kind and generous in all you do,
And when others behave badly,
become sweet and mellow,
Say with love, "tease all you want," for…

I'm Special—This, I Know

A Fish Tail's Tale
"Somethin's Fishy"

———————

Now, here comes a story that's rather deep,
For out of the depths of the ocean, it did seep,
In fact, it came on the back of a crab as it did creep,
And when I read it, my tears flowed; it made me weep,
Weep however, with joy, and more,
It is a tale that everyone should lock away;
it's one to store,
A school of fish had a leader rare,
It could only swim backwards, as none other would dare,
Dare not, to say the least,
For when he was born,
the other fish beasts thought of him, as a feast,
But he fooled them all,
He learned to live with his strange fate;
he had a 'fish-ball,'
He was born with only one eye,
And that is not the worst;
it was located above his tail, aye,
So in order to see where he was going,
he had to swim in reverse,
The other members of the school became grumpy,
some even terse,
Most wanted that little 'one-eye' to leave,
But others, who had more heart,
said that they would grieve,
So, he was accepted, and giggled with glee,
After all,

149

he was able to swim with the school, and see,
But sometimes,
he would become quite playful, and turn around,
Turn around, and turn around,
and turn around, like a merry-go-round,
Can you just picture the seahorses going up and down?
Then, he grew up, became quite renowned,
For when other "fishies" saw him swimming tail end first,
They were jealous; it gave them a great thirst,
His tail could wipe away anything that came his way,
It was like a human's windshield wiper on the sway,

Debris would fly; no need to blink, even if he could,
He, on occasion,
became the leader of the pack; that they understood,
For suddenly one day,
when no one expected anything to arise,
A ferocious storm came along wrapped in a disguise,
It whipped up the ocean floor,
and battered each fish in the school,
It was so masterful, and so unthinking and so cruel,
But somehow,
little one-eye instinctively knew what to do,
His windshield wiper tail, really flew,
And he found safe haven for his family in a cave,
He became their hero; he was so brave,
That nasty storm was whippin' winds
against his face,
It did not know his eye was in another place,
A place they could not see,
So, he was able to go along and flee,
To find a spot where all could rest,
It was in times like these that he was at his best,
And when the storm left,
he was crowned the new leader,

In fact, they named him,
Abraham Moses Peter,
He swam at the head of the school,
his tail end up front,
Other fish schools thought he was just pulling a stunt,
Little did they know
how important one-eye had become,
His giggle was a signal for his school
to act frolicsome,
Now, what can fish do to create some fun troubles?
They would, all together, giggle,
creating hundreds of bubbles,
That in turn, would tickle the flesh
of the fish in the other school,
After all, there was no, 'no giggle rule,'
So you see even fish learn in school, underground,
Rightly so, for that is where they can be found,
But there is one thing they cannot do - drool,
But I will bet they all live by the 'Golden Rule,'
Especially the giants of the deep; the shark and whale,
And now you know, the story of

A Fish Tail's Tale
"SOMETHIN'S FISHY"

Time Is Life

Time is life,
Beat a drum; tickle a fife,
Be sad, be happy, be always on the move,
We do not count our seconds;
they come and go, self-remove,
Life is but a millisecond of time's history,
It is nothing but a half-blink;
nothing but a mystery,
How and where did time begin?
We invaded it's space, joined its march –
much to our chagrin,
For we fade and time moves on,
Does time have an end,
its own great beyond?
How much time does time have to live;
does it live in a time wave?
Does it die within each life it lives;
within the existence it gave?
Can it simply be defined as perpetual motion?
I do not have a notion,
It is constantly moving,
without measurable calm or strife,
It is consistent – defines our being…

Time Is Life

"??????????"

What do I propose?
Nothing. There it goes,
Let it run, let it run,
Let it run and then some,
What could that be?
Every day it gets away from me,
And then I smile,
I know it will stop, after a while,
But for now let it run; let it run,
Let it run, let it run, and then some,
It has its own plan; and there it goes,
It wipes away joyful moments and woes,
It heals in its own way,
It has nothing, and yet, a lot to say,
Let it run, let it run,
Let it run, and then some,
It can be stopped only by its creator,
I would surmise,
And only stops running when everything dies,
And what is this thing that runs so well,
and sounds like a crime?
It is not, you know;
it is the crux of our life – it is...

Time!

Your Mind

Does the human mind control our powers
of concentration?
Or, do our powers of concentration control,
and rule our mind, a form of liberation?

What is the mind?
Consciousness, thoughts,
Intellect, memory for mankind,
Animals and such are beyond my reach,
Communications are nil;
I know not their patterns of speech,
But I do know, the mind is a magnificent tool,
Working 24 hours a day, awake and asleep, it can rule,
It needs to be treated with tender loving care,
As it runs through its peaks and valleys,
with its good and bad to share,
It needs to be nourished;
fed the right thoughts and ways,
So it can function smoothly; throughout its days,
So each life will have the strength it needs to survive,
Without short circuits; be as alive, as a bee hive,
Be full of the art of concentration and decision making,
From each moment of its day is in its waking,
For the mind determines right and wrong –
good and bad,
Through all periods of normal and 'mad,'
It can shut down, or be open for all to see,
That's why one must always use the mind correctly,

Say no more, let it be; remember it is there,
Where? Where it should be?
You tell me,
Under the skull, above and behind the face,
That's where it belongs; so keep it in its place,
Treat it with respect; concentrate on being kind,
Protect at all costs your body's precious power plant...

Your Mind

Feelin' Good

I finished my 20 Easter cards
with notes and poems enclosed,
How good I feel to have accomplished
the task; to myself, I crowed,
That's not all I did today,
And tomorrow is well on its way,
So, off to bed I will go,
With a promise to myself – "no crow,"
Just a wonderful, peaceful sleep,
Without having to count sheep,
For I finished what I should,
I'm content, and

Feelin' Good

(Goodnight!)

Life's Clock

Tick, Tock, Tick, Tock, Tick, Tock,
Good morning,
Tick, Tock, Tick, Tock,
Good night,
Tick, Tock, Tick, Tock,
Good morning,
Tick, Tock,
Good night,
N'est-ce pas?
(Isn't that so?)

Good morning,
Good night,
Tick, Tock, Tick, Tock
Tick, Tock,
Tick, Tick, Tick, Tick,

TICK

Words

"Words, where have you gone?"
You're the ones I depend upon,
I feel alone, lost; walking among giant desert dunes,
on an empty, endless shore,
I see a peculiar mirage; no house, just a door,
Why would I open it, when I can walk around?
Can any sense in that picture, be found?
It's almost like having an empty head,
Or, one crammed with thoughts that can't be read,
Like skeletons in a closet waiting to be released,
Rattling until their owners become deceased,
Words, how important, crucial, you are,
Without you, expressions are lost
hiding on some galaxy star,
To live on in a distant forever,
To be shared, never,
Just a dream,
A distant sun beam,
Then I think of nature;
it can communicate in silence,
In a vacuum of sound abstinence,
But, it can come alive with twittering,
chirping birds,
And so can we because of ...

Words

'Time for bed; time to sleep – give up your words;
give up your thoughts so profoundly deep'

Goodbye

Oh, youth of old you fickle thing,
How could you leave me to join another's fling?
That's not nice you know?
To leave me floundering so,
"Aren't you ashamed, you dirty bird?"
I guess my goose is cooked,
for want of another word,
I know from those who lived in the past,
you won't be back,
I am on my own, but do not worry,
I will find a new track,
My youth may be gone,
But I have stored some treasures,
You cannot take away all my life long pleasures,
So 'goodbye' my youth of old,
Do not come back; remember, my tent won't fold,
There is plenty going on inside,
My life's aggregate wide,
Go ahead, join the frivolous…flit and fly,
But do not come back; you forgot to say,

Goodbye

What's In Your Closet?

Dark? Dust?
Damp? Mold?
Clothes? Shoes? Glasses? Dishes?
Or, skeletons hidden by somebody's wishes?
I am sure many things have been gathering
rust and dust for years,
Except the skeletons, they stay clean
for instant release; washed by tears,
Actually, closets are very interesting places,
to say the least,
In many cases,
they hide the unwanted; hold a mental feast,
Many a body has rolled out of a closet,
during a game of hide and seek,
And many a gift-hunter has found gold; stole a peek,
Closets are great around Holiday time; they are
packed to expanding,
And when empty, they become quite demanding,
They are just holes in the walls,
Most forget what they have stored
in these good ole clothes stalls,
If you are lucky, you will own a walk-in,
However, in most you will get stuck,
unless you are quite thin,
This is a whimsical topic – approached just for fun,
Now, I suggest you check your closets; walk do not run,

You may just have enough room to hang a sign ...
"SPACE-TO-LET,"
So be prepared the next time you are asked..........

What's In Your Closet?

Bowls

And I'm not talking about the ones
upon which you place your cheeks,
No, it's the ones that accept your morning
fare; for example the one that speaks,
The one that snaps, crackles, and pops,
The others that lose their taste, when stale
become limp, flip-flops,
Where would they all be
without the milk to swim in and upon?
And without the wheat,
corn, oats, and rice; woe be gone,
How much interest would there be without
those many flavors?
And the various enhancements like salt and fat
and sugar, for the 'little shavers?'
Oh, yes, how about the sizes and shapes – letters
and faces, puffs and trolls?
And, oh, my, just think how messy breakfast
would be without simple …

Bowls

How About?

How about soup without a dish?
Or, a star upon which we can wish?
How about a face without a nose?
Or feet, with lengthy finger toes?
How about shoes to accommodate that change?
Sizes would be different; shoemakers would
have to provide a new range,
How about a head with only one ear?
Or, one with two mouths;
I must admit, that I would fear,
'How about?' is almost as profound as "What if?"
How about the challenge of a newly found hieroglyph,
That should stimulate an archeologist'
appetite better than any aperitif,
How about a constant
forever gardenia fragrance; want a wiff?
How about noting that our "what ifs?"
and "how abouts" will rise
like souls in the end,
It is inevitable; we will have to leave some
with a younger friend,
But do not ever throw any questions out,
They have life ad infinitum, particularly...
"why?" "what if?" and

How About?

We Are Today

We are not yesterday,
We are today!
We are not tomorrow,
Unless, we live to
fill the time given to that day,
The Universe is expanding,
We are shrinking,
Tomorrow
will be found in that expansion,
It's not within our day,
Tomorrow can never really be today,
Can it?
Today cannot be yesterday,
Just as yesterday cannot be today,
Nor should it be,
We can only live in today,
Never yesterday, nor tomorrow,
And in relationship to
all our known yesterdays,

Comparatively speaking, isn't each total life
simply a matter of a minute
in comparison to known time and all creation?

We are not yesterday,
We are not tomorrow,

We Are Today

Smile & Wink

I must be quick,
It's not a trick,
I have but 15 minutes
to say something bright,
It is time to go to bed; it is night,
And I hate to let the day slip away,
But I have not written a poem yet, for today,
Fail to follow a promise to me,
That's to write a poem-a-day you see,
So, here it is — short and sweet,
I did follow through; I had a deadline to meet,
But this is pushing procrastination
to its limit; don't ya think?
Not to worry, I will finish in no time, then

Smile & Wink

My Socks

---※---

Thank God, I'm not a centipede;
I'm having problems with my socks,
They are all too short and tight
on the ankle; what crocks,
Shouldn't the heel come around and fit tight?
Well, they do not; and they give me quite a fight,
They come up on the leg, if they're so inclined,
They all seem to express their own mind,
And *"one size fits all"* forget it; that simply mocks,
Any color, any size, they're all the same – trouble;
and they are mine…

My Socks

Life Has A Fragrance All Its Own

Yes, life has a fragrance all its own,
It can be found in every second you have ever known,
It's in the air,
Do you care?
Where you go,
You grow,
Whatever you do,
You grow,
When you think,
When you blink,
Your life has changed,
Your senses are rearranged,
With every breath, there's an
instinctive fragrance of that time, that place,
A passerby can change the air within your space,
You know when someone is near,
The fragrance of their life and time would be clear,
When you talk,
You grow,
When you walk,
You grow,
Life is special; it became more your own,
With each step, you've grown,
But overall, for all, not matter what – remember...

Life Has A Fragrance All Its Own

Speak To Me

Speak to me, oh, my mind, unwind,
Let cascading thoughts flow; what will I find?
Treasures hidden deep within my subconscious world,
Let them spin like tops; let them be unraveled, 'un-twirled,'
I want to think more clearly, know myself better; be absolute,
Be definite in theory, thought, and words; be free to execute,
Find a way to express the inner me,
Not while I sleep in dreams and fantasy,
No, wide awake absorb the living,
To see what the world is offering,
at this very minute; what is it giving?
I wonder, after death, will we dream?
Or, will our spirits remain at rest – ever serene?
So many questions,
so few answers, so little time; don't you agree?
With an endless desire,
I plead to the world, my mind, and the great beyond…

Speak To Me

The Perfect Sleeping Pill

It's amazing – falling asleep at will,
This invention is better than any sleeping pill,
An electronic tube with programs dull,
Program, after program – exercises in awful,
The news of the day
is repeated and repeated, ad nauseam,
The same details, from different mouths, ad infinitum,
It's like eating a jar of pickles – not sweet, dill,
It puts you right into 'slumber land,' it's…

The Perfect Sleeping Pill

Please Don't Communicate

Why should I want to communicate with you?
Seems a funny question, but sometimes it's true,
You wait and wait, and wait to hear,
Particularly, from those who you miss, and hold dear,
Then again, it could be a matter of a business venture,
Waiting to finalize paperwork, to begin a new adventure,
Checking the mailbox for word from those traveling afar,
Waiting for an answer – did I make the grade, pass the bar?
So the comment really does not apply,
when said, "I can wait,"
When it is facetiously stated, as…

Please Don't Communicate

Introspective Silence

Some of life's most telling moments come,
when I turn myself on me,
When I delve deep within that raging
and calming inner sea,
Preys tell what will I share; what will I steal?
What inner part of me do I ever want to reveal?
Walking in a forest without a breeze,
You can search your inner self with ease,
Walking alone on a quiet road or down a lane,
You can see yourself as looking out a window pane,
Life passes quickly; you can recall all you've done,
You can answer your own feelings
prickly sweet; you are the only one,
How much did I hate; how much did I love?
How many times did I follow the devil's angels; my
God's angels from above?
Why was I foolish and selfish, when I acted so?
Where was my heart; on an arrow in a bow?
Did I ever not acknowledge an outstretched hand?
To remember, my mind must search its depths –
those mental dunes on the desert sand,
Search a lake, drink in its shimmering moon,
where rests my own self-defense,
Will I ever come to know my own level of intense; my
own level of...

Introspective Silence

A Hug

'ANOTHER BLESSING FROM ABOVE'

Our first hug is a temporary 'goodbye,'
As we leave our home in the eternal sky,
When God caresses our soul,
and places it in the care of another,
To be warm, snug, nurtured inside
the one you will love and call, 'Mother,'
And for a very short time
you will be hugged 24 hours a day,
Then gently coaxed - nudged to join the world –
be on your way,
Hugged by your Mother's arms, held in quiet peace,
Until of course you scream; ask, no, plead for release,
Year-in and year-out, the hugs gain greater meaning,
Later, your memory will recall
and reel out that love you were gleaning,
Hugs to keep you warm, heal a hurt, say 'thank you,'
or recognize a job well done,
Those hugs reserved for 'special people,'
'special occasions' – hugs for one,
How quickly we learn;
the one with the greatest 'hug store' is a Mother,
The one, who innately anticipates,
without being prodded, the needs of another,

The one who has mastered the art of sharing love,
Who has been blessed with grace by angels above,
The one who understands without question
the desperation in a simple 'tug,'
And knows the true meaning in giving and receiving ...

A Hug

Time Determines Its Own
'TICK TOCK'
TIME SETS ITS OWN PACE

Why is time in such a hurry?
We scurry here; we scurry there, and like the
world around, we scurry, scurry, scurry,
Where are we all going?
Step aside – watch the traffic and people flowing;
they just keep flowing, flowing, flowing,
Actually, its constant syncopation;
time in motion,
Time living in tune with the
ebb and flow of the ocean,
Time riding a breeze,
a gale, or on a gentle wind,
Time is nothing less than perpetual motion –
with kinetic momentum,
Time has no time to swing left and right on a
pendulum or wait for a clock's, tintinnabulum,
It travels in only one direction,
forward – never back,
And we ride its wave from first light of birth
'til death's black,
We cannot question time's way,
Although we live within its grasp, day
after day, after day,
Time flies, and we fly with it too,
And to keep pace, we move on,

doing whatever we have to do,
That is why it doesn't pay to watch a clock;
forget the clock,

Time Determines Its Own
'TICK TOCK'
TIME SETS ITS OWN PACE

175

Hey, Who Is In Control?

'Mind & Body; No, Body & Mind'

A wonderful question that –
Someone has to be in control;
that's where it's at,
But when it comes to mind and body
the rules are changed,
Particularly, if the mind becomes deranged,
Or when it insists the body do something
it physically cannot,
Or when the body simply forgot,
What a twosome 'mind & body;'
okay, okay, 'body & mind,'
Let's not get ornery; let's not be unkind,
Only one can be first at any given time,
And when it happens, it's really not a crime,
Who is in control; you know when you cannot move?
You just have to wait for things to
resolve and improve,
Today, it could be the body; it can't go,
Tomorrow, the mind is fuzzy; so?
But, if they both crash; simultaneously fall,
You just wait; you've been put on recall,
There are times, when mind & body function
in opposition,

Neither is in control and that is not supposition,
That is when you wish you had a negotiating troll,
And you cannot stop yelling...

Hey, Who Is In Control?

Laughter And A
Twinkle In An Eye

Laughter and a twinkle in an eye,
They go together, like twinkling stars in the sky,
I wonder, when stars twinkle,
are they laughing – filled with glee?
If so, what a happy bunch they must be,
Perhaps they are laughing at
what they see down below,
Millions of earth's wee things
crawling and running to and fro,
A world of motion –
some actually getting somewhere,
While others, trapped in a motion so slow,
they simply stare,
Where is everyone going in such a hurry?
The stars must have surely renamed the Earth –
'The Land of Scurry,'
How often of late, have you caught
laughter and a twinkle in an eye?
There isn't much time for that
in our present state of 'Fly,'
That is why I so enjoy a
twinkle in the eye of a mischievous child,
The lighthearted innocence
ignoring seriousness, running wild,
Their land of joy is so different from ours,
They look for worms and creepy bugs on

flowers – for hours,
They do not have the worries created
by those who look after them,
Those providing the 'must have' gems
from which all worries stem,
That is why I find joy in nature; the oceans ripples,
squirrels chasing round a tree, the stars in the sky,
It's all around, so close to see and hear, like
laughter and a twinkle in an eye

Until It's Done

'IT'S JUST BEGUN'

The dark of night & light of day
graced the *Earth* long before I,
The sun and moon roamed among the stars,
eons before it was called sky
Who knows what happened to each planet in flight?
Why they are as they are, cold, hot, dull and bright?
How can the sun harbor heat so rare and intense?
And be the size it is – gigantic, immense?
How many millions of things have emerged
and disappeared without our knowledge?
Who has recorded every wave
that found a water's edge?
Does anyone know the numbers of feathers on
every bird that ever lived and died?
How many snowflakes and raindrops have fallen from
angel eyes that cried?
What are we, compared to all that has come and gone
over the course of time?
No life is long enough to understand
the Creator's level of sublime,
And in death will we find all the answers once sought?
Will the knowledge then be useless, all for naught?
Who can we tell, now that we know the
greatest mystery of all, about life after death?
Who knows how much air to date
has been needed to support each breath?
How many grains of sand cover the *World's* ground?
How much remains to be unearthed – to be found?
So much to be learned and

so little time in which to learn it,
But, oh, the joy to be part of the process –
keep the flame lit,
How tall the tower of knowledge today,
How tall, and it has just begun to find its way,
For each age builds upon the prior one,
Where will it end? We will never know –

Until It's Done

Why An Itch Deserves A Scratch

'If for nothing less, its indefatigableness'...Jeanette Dowdell

An itch is the most persistent irritant I know,
And if gently placated,
it might just take a hike, and go,
You cannot zap an itch,
like an annoying, buzzing bug,
But, you sure can answer back
with a scratch, or a shrug,
The worst of all these mighty devils is
the one you cannot reach,
Doorframes, backscratchers, sticks
don't satisfy the little 'beeech,'
I believe persistence like the squeaky wheel
must be met head-on,
With whatever means it takes,
besides yelling, 'Oh, be gone,'
So, my little itch,
I give you credit, you little witch,
For driving me crazy,
making my skin crawl, and twitch,
Have you ever felt the sting of a simple switch?
That would be the final blow,
For that would hurt me more, you know?
An ostrich I will not become,
And persistence renders you – not dumb,
So let's negotiate, one 'itch' to another,
For right now, I have one word,

one thought for you; it is 'smother,'
I give you credit, but will not give in,
by admitting, I've met my match,
For what it's worth,
I am telling the world just …

Why An Itch Deserves A Scratch

How Deep The Love, How Deep

How deep the heart, how deep the soul,
how deep the forgiveness goes,
How sweet, how deep, how rich and warm,
steady as melodic oboes,
It is in the smile; it is in the eyes and hugs – ever gold,
And yet, God did not create them all in the same mold,
How different they are, one from the other,
And believe me, they know
whether they deserve to be called 'mother,'
Everyone else's needs and desires come first,
Hers remain suppressed; she waits to satisfy that thirst,
How intense, how poignant,
the obvious joy they find in giving,
Other's success and happiness, gives them reason for living,
Not to have known that deep level of love
leaves a portion of one in an abyss,
For through good times and bad
that characteristic can only raise one to a state of bliss,
Love eases the sorrow, eases the hurt, eases the pain,
How deep the inner reserves; it shows, its plain,
To be a mother comes with a price quite steep,
If you can feel and understand the rewards; then you know...

How Deep The Love, How Deep

Oh, Mighty Curse

It itches, it burns, it cracks the skin,
It has got to be the devil breaking
out from within,
Has my life been filled with nothing but sin?
I look at my hands, red and raw,
and see the devil with a grin,
Morning and noon, and all day through;
'Take a hike,' I say,
For now it is night; time to pray,
I will ask forgiveness, as I always do,
And ask again, for relief from the likes of you,
It is not getting any better; it is getting worse,
'Be gone, Oh, be gone,

Oh, Mighty Curse

Our Circle

I walked the circle round,
But it was incomplete I found,
The beginning and end points did not yet meet,
But that meeting is not of our choosing,
not one we can beat,
Life's circle is actually a life clock,
It meters out each moment,
with each tick, each tock,
And we walk not knowing it's there,
Doing our thing – totally unaware,
Until one day, it slows to a creep,
And professional help we must seek,
The inner works are wearing out,
We lived it, as we wished no doubt,
But now,
pieces are flaking off; slowly, but well defined,
Activities go, as we assume more frequently,
positions of reclined,
And,
the two points of our circle have each other in sight,
Their meeting depends upon their magnetic might,
And so we struggle to break
the magnetism as best we can,
Hold tight to what we have left;
keep it as close as when it began,
But the ultimate goal of our two points in life

is to eventually meet,
And we will know when it is time for them to so greet,
Take a walk down memory lane, now draped in purple,
Soon it will be time to say, 'Goodbye,'
when we complete...

Our Circle

Why?

Can we not be a planet within a planet? I wonder,
Can we not be a star within a star –
or a black hole ready to break asunder?
Actually, what do we really know?
A little of this, a little of that;
how far will our creator let us go?
We lean and build on what was done before,
We walk through someone else's open door,
We live within the shadows of geniuses
who graced many a prior era,
Within their world, within their genre,
Who is to say there is not a planet within our planet,
filled with alien "hot shots?"
True creatures of the deep, non-human zealots,
Driving our wills to perform our life's deeds,
Filling us at will with their thoughts and seeds?
The point is, we will never know everything
no matter how hard we try,
We are human, not God; that is why we will always ask,

Why?

Trauma

Would you like to venture a guess?
Which life events create the greatest stress?
There are so many from which to choose,
And, if you pick the wrong one, what will I lose?
I believe it has to be love,
The one that creates a deep, crushing void;
that is what I am speaking of,
That trauma; it takes the wind right out of the sails,
But life goes on; emotion gives way and reason prevails,
The loss of a loved one;
the loss of a promised forever love,
Changes our ways, our perspective on life;
but we learn to rise above,
Grief, injury, and sickness, they too take their toll,
These are the traumas of life that strengthen one's soul,
With the help of others, we do survive,
We remold ourselves and move on – grateful to be alive,
'This too shall pass,' becomes an inner mantra
Whenever the pain burns deep in any personal...

Trauma

Stubborn

I am stubborn; I was born that way,
That is not a characteristic
I am proud to possess, convey,
I do not believe it can be learned or taught,
And it is not one actively sought,
Who wants to be stubborn? Not, me,
I would rather be tenacious; don't you agree?
That might wear off, down the road,
But stubbornness is an unchangeable mode,
Even my hair is as stubborn as I,
I will comb it to the left and the
next thing I know, it turns right in reply,
I am quite aware of this innate trait,
To change is like making all clocks
run backwards; it is an uncontrolled fate,
Do I care? Yes, I do,
It can make others uncomfortable too,
I often fight to overcome nature's way,
'Let it go' – 'Let it go;' in my mind,
that is what I say,
But, I will usually stand firm,
Even though that inflexibility makes me squirm,
All things are very difficult to overturn
When one is born
and known to have a streak of the...

Stubborn

For The Light Of Day

When I awake each morn,
I am grateful for the sight of dawn,
And the early morning bird songs,
My first stretch; my first yawn,
"Hurray for me - hurray, for another day!'"
It is precious. " Use it well," I say,
How many do not have that gift unfurled?
How many do not recognize its value, throughout
the world?
How many do not care if the sun should rise?
How many walk through the hours
with their life in disguise,
Pretense; life is just there, theirs to be had,
And the clock moves on – nothing special; how sad.
To me
every breath I breathe is worth the effort,
I would not want the giver of life to feel
I would like to give it back – mission abort,
Remember,
no matter how sly the thief, he cannot steal time,
Nor can he borrow what is yours and mine,
For me, no matter what it holds; I will always pray,
Look up, reach out each morning, and say...
thank you, God,

For The Light Of Day

Good!

If I had to do it over again, I would
Try to do better, if I could,
But then didn't I do my best, as I should?
Sounds good to me – real good!

Good!

Extremely Elusive

Why can't I find the life I want to live?
Why does it elude me;
like water through a sieve?
The answer is simple;
I really do not know what I want,
For if I did, it would be mine and abundant,
Did I ever know in life
what I thought would be best for me?
Or, were all my goals simply illusionary?
Were there too many others directing my will;
deciding my fate?
Why did I not end up as others
with children and a mate?
Why did my life's steps go the way they did?
I was born like everyone else, a pot without a lid,
Did I stifle my own freedom to do?
I don't think so – do you?
How would you know,
you would have to have lived my 70 plus years,
Live them with all their joys and sorrows – laughter and tears,
And now, I am on the downside of the slippery slope,
Still scratching and clawing and yelling... "Throw me a rope,"
I am still reaching for the top of the mountain – its peak,
Will I ever find what I am looking for; what I seek?
No, today, I want this; yesterday, I wanted that,

My mind's like an old fashioned 'Automat,'
Someday,
I might settle in, although it is not conclusive,
For life's dreams are always the same for me,

Extremely Elusive

Yesterday Is Gone

Yesterday is gone,
Where did it go?
Like the phantom of the human spirit,
it was whisked away,
Which moments will fade into mystery?
Which will remain indelible – become history?

Yesterday is gone,
Would you like to bring it back?

Today is here,
Live a memory,

For it too will soon disappear, like the day and the night,
And once again we'll say with surprise,

Yesterday Is Gone
(Where did it go?)

And The Battle Goes On

I have looked at others fighting themselves within,
Wanting to escape, yet, living their chagrin,
Feeling trapped;
not knowing really what they want to do,
They created the struggle they live; their own code blue,
They cannot find a way,
or know how to begin to change their fate,
So they wait for something to happen;
they stall – they wait,
And life moves on, but theirs stands still,
They keep hoping 'tomorrow' will direct their inner will,
And the battle goes on, but nothing new comes along,
They keep singing the same refrain from their favorite song,
It's a terrible thing to be trapped within oneself,
Waiting for someone else to recognize their need –
perhaps a genie, or an elf,
No, the inner-self must be pushed into
a detour to find release,
We cannot wait for someone else to see what we feel
or wait for the pressure to suddenly decrease,
We must find the answer; and then
to ourselves announce, 'self-doubt is gone,'
Otherwise, precious times escape, float away on air...

And The Battle Goes On

Why Cheat? Why Steal? Why Lie?

If you can't succeed on your own, you're 'small fry,'
'Small potatoes,' not worth your weight
in any metal; you didn't try,
You had to take something that you didn't earn,
And for eternity your soul is sure to burn,
You're not worth the breath given to you at birth,
You'll always be what you are without value, without worth,
So go ahead, rob and steal,
Reduce yourself to Satan's level; you'll be his tasty meal,
Forever you'll burn in the fire of hell,
Go ahead, cheat and lie; someone knows and will surely tell,
Without your help, your secret will out,
You'll live your life with everyone's doubt,
You'll lose your self-respect; you'll no longer be trusted,
Once you become known for what you are; you'll be busted,
If you're not satisfied with what you've got,
Go out and earn what you feel is your lot, otherwise
go to hell and rot,
With decent folks, your style won't fly,
Too bad you never asked yourself...

Why Cheat? Why Steal? Why Lie?

Pitter-Patter

Raindrops, raindrops, raindrops, pitter-patter,
pitter-patter, pitter-patter,
What's wrong with that? What's the matter?
We need the rain, we do,
Otherwise, the rain barrel will never be full,
The ground will crack and cry for a drink,
How can we water one cup at a time from the sink,
And if it does not rain, the tap will run dry,
Then the prayers will have to fly,
Things all around will wilt and fade,
Waterfalls will no longer cascade,
The old adage will hold true,
You won't miss 'it,' until it's not there for you,
So do feel blest when it rains, be grateful for the pitter-patter,
in the singing rains' refrains,
And recognize that nothing is the matter,
As long as we hear each downpour's...

Pitter-Patter

What Is Time?

We are time,
We are its prime,
Each moment we live
represents proof of its existence,
For we do not exist in its absence,
Do we?

The Shining

The moon shines,
The sun shines,
The stars shine,
And we, on their reflections, dine,
Esthetically,
Magically,
Leeches of nature; so refine,
We wait for the lights to feed
our need; our desire,
They provide the atmosphere for our goals;
those to which we aspire,
If the lights we take for granted leave,
We would be more than pining,
Why do we not recognize,
we would fast fade without

"The Shining"

Time To Say Goodbye

It is never a good time to say, "Goodbye,"
Unless of course, something is going awry,
But when it involves a deep love,
you must let go,
That makes the adrenalin flow, and flow,
The heart quickens and emotions present their case,
Hasten the moment; there's no time to waste,
For tears will flow and you will wear
your feelings on your sleeve,
Just go; please go - just leave,
Very often it's said, "Parting is such sweet sorrow,"
Not in my book; never –
whether yesterday, today, or tomorrow,
It is always clear to me;
I do not want to say, 'Goodbye,'
The pain runs deep and I never can answer, why?
Even though I know they will come back,
But the time between now and then,
throws me off track,
And when it involves a final farewell;
should something or someone die,
There is never, no never, a good

Time To Say Goodbye

Misty Moments

Memories manufacture misty moments,
They conjure up angels and serpents,
They unveil life's joys and sorrows,
To memory, yesterdays are a must;
but it cannot touch tomorrows,
That's why we should rarely look back,
Look ahead to where memories will be born;
open the door just a crack,
Set out your goals; peek at your dreams,
Enjoy shining moments bathed in the sunbeams,
There can be no furrows in tomorrow's light,
It represents the new unmarred,
untarnished world,
Oh, things will happen tomorrow,
when their time is ripe,
But today is not the time to identify
black crepe moments of any type,
You have to live and give; try and fail,
to truly enjoy success when it comes,
Overcome the
'fearsome' to revel in the 'gladsomes,'
For through it all, as one lives, every
yesterday becomes a tomorrow – memory event,
And if lived to the fullest,
emotional times will always be filled with

Misty Moments

Stars And Sand

Scientists have determined that there are more stars
than all the earth's grains of sand,
I wonder who and when, they began to count, and
if their lives can be found in a world called…'expand,'
Can't you picture them sitting and counting each grain
of sand under bodies of water and on the surface of earth?
I am sure they began many millennia before their birth,
And how many times did they have to begin again,
Try another whole chorus and refrain,
When a strong current or blustery wind changed the count,
And when it reached a number beyond which we are
aware; how did they that challenge surmount?
Who whispers in their ears,
"Go ahead, start again, my 'Sisyphean' friend,"
Nature is your job security; your job will never end,
So I query this, 'While you are counting grains of sand;
who is counting the stars?'
Are they traveling along the 'Champs de Mars?'
Don't forget, our starry 'Milky Way' is not a candy bar,
Squelch all those earthly thoughts; catch a shooting star,
For millions could be born while the counting is in progress,
I'm not only in awe of the idea, but its conclusion, I confess,
This conclusion and its plan reach far beyond grand,
So I sit… a star in one hand,
a grain of sand in the other, and contemplate,

Stars And Sand

Just Thinking

I am having some 'what if' thoughts,
odd ones to be sure,
Thoughts that come from the negative moments
we have to endure,
Actually, the deep seeded feelings
found in moments of loss,
The loss of loved ones, a job, being second best
in the eyes of your boss,
We are expected to accept these moments,
and more, with grace,
But, 'what if' our society's dictates, we don't embrace?
Why do I have to say, or accept the comment,
'Perhaps it was meant to be'
'Oh, yeah,' let's just say, 'Oh, fiddle-dee-dee,'
Why do I, like some sheep, have to fall in line?
This is my life, not societies'; it's mine!
And yet to survive, one must do, what one must do,
Like it or not, if you do not fall in line
you are very often through,
To me, life is just a charade,
No one is different, no matter how hard they try;
they are just odd,
They do not fit in, so they become the 'odd-ball out,'
In either scenario, they do not live in a world of clout,
Loners are just that – loners,
They have to live with themselves;

they become their only owners,
You see, 'what if' can be amazing, amusing,
even, sometimes – stinking,
When I fall without notice
into a quizzical mood, one of...

Just Thinking

The Intolerable

Sir Winston Churchill said it best,
He found aging to be 'intolerable' –
no doubt, hard to digest,
How astute, how profound, how right on,
The trappings of the body hang on its frame,
but its life is gone,
The mind wanders down memory lane,
Torments the spirit; reminding it,
it has nothing to gain,
But the human will is a powerful tool,
And try as old age may,
it will not accept the role of fool,
The mind and body no longer agree,
Yesterday's clump together for support
as they drift off to sea,
Floating further away,
yet always keeping in touch,
Because their memory
represents a life and can mean so much,
What meant so much then
rarely means much as we age,
Time rewrites each life as it moves along –
by simply recording another page,
And before the story can be told, it might reach its end,
For who can tell it better than the one who
made the moments blend?
And very often, before anyone ever has a chance
to say, 'Goodbye; they are gone,

Gone forever — they will have moved on,
After all, isn't that the part that is the most incalculable?
Before we reach the painless portion promised,
we all must tolerate...

The Intolerable

I Just Don't Comprehend

I *just* don't comprehend,
Life, and Death, a candle wick's beginning and end,
At birth the wick is set aflame,
We are set on a course; given a name,
And what goes on from there, until the flame goes out?
It is called life,
most filled with some surety and many a doubt,
In the course of history, it is but a bubble on the sea,
Quickly born, quickly lived, quickly does it flee,
That is why so many live with such ferocity,
Why not, gentleness, with a little more veracity?
So much more would be accomplished for the good,
Perhaps peace would reign; we would reach
the ultimate point of 'understood,'
Yes, the wick burns on, the candle
is in a constant state of melt,
And each moment that passes presses on
heartfelt,
We all want life to go on as we know it now,
Why would anyone want to face death,
the uncertain, the unknown, anyhow?
Life is a mystery, until it unfolds,
Death is a deeper mystery;
no one knows what it holds,
No one living, that is,
Perhaps the answer is in our souls, that's the answer – so it 'tis,
For in the beginning, the soul is lighted with life's wick,
The spiritual, immortal, undefined – maverick,

It is virgin in its beginning,
but can it be the same at the end?
It is part of both, life and death; could they be
one in the same? That's what...

I Just Don't Comprehend

Before We Must Leave It Behind

The clock is ticking and ticking,
and ticking; time is moving on,
And here I sit on the edge of the bed, watching the hands
move the seconds and minutes; then they are gone,
You cannot stop time; it is life's measuring rod,
From beginning to end, it is in the hands of God,
I did not ask in my beginning, 'Where am I going?'
But I do now, 'What am I reaping? What am I sowing?
I ask – over, and over, and over again,
When the clock stops, what then?
An historical mystery, unanswered;
as deep as death's forever,
It is always time to tally the aggregate
of each life's endeavor,
Each day, life moves at its own pace,
Takes us from dawn to dawn
within an unchanging set space,
Twenty-four hours, fourteen hundred
and forty minutes set aside for each day,
Multiply that by your age; and you might ask,
'Where does time go anyway?'
It goes where it has gone, down through the ages,
It disappears like life's wages,
Time is the invisible vapor trail
that defines a human's existence,
Even though it is there, it is simply
artificial phosphorescence,
We don't see time's light, but it's there –

burning away each day,
We never think of it dying out – giving way,
And that is as it should be,
Yet, somewhere deep within,
we should recognize life's absurdity,
Life is but a myth – borrowed and
lived one breath at a time,
That is why wasting time is such a crime,
Never watch a clock or listen to its ticking,
without something in mind,
It is the banquet on which we feast...

Before We Must Leave It Behind

An Ad Infinitum Glow

———————

Don't deny me quiet moments
with spirits of the past,
Their generosity and love make
their memories last,
None are as far away as most seem to think;
hard to retrieve,
Not if you recognize and feel their presence; simply believe,
That is part of what I know as life everlasting;
life remaining forever,
Their love is part of your spirit,
as yours will be part of someone else's – leaving never,
And so, it moves along in an eternal flow,
Ever shining, like the stars above, with

An Ad Infinitum Glow

My Friendship Genealogy Tree

When I die, I want to leave my mark,
invisible and free,
Like dogs leave their marks, wherever they pee,
But, funny thing,
they do not have to a leave a mark;
it is in your heart – their eternal loyalty,
And that is the mark,
I want to leave on

My Friendship Genealogy Tree

What Is Time?

Does it have a beginning?
Does it have an end?
Who created time?
Is God time?
Is time endless?
Does time actually exist?
What does timeless really mean?
Where is time?
Does time ever rest?
Why is time called time?

What Is Time?

Tears, Tears, Tears

The firefighters of life,
They ease pain,
They release anger and joy,
They say many times
what words cannot convey,
Whatever would we be without them?
Fires would rage and burn, even
our souls would turn to cinders,
Whoever thinks about the purpose they serve?
Until one cries and you hear, 'Let it all out,'
Yes, it is good to let whatever
you are harboring loose,
Let the world deal with your tears,
They are no less than another non-word for feelings,
Are they not synonymous with emotions?
Tears rarely form when invoking reason
But they are, and will remain,
the firefighters of life,

Tears, Tears, Tears

Special Enough To Give Me A Fit

Soft rain, a day to call its own,
Falling free, quietly making its presence known,
I wonder if each drop was touched
by a ray of sunlight,
Would it shine in a rainbow glow, ever bright?
How beautiful would that be?
A rainbow falling in drops, falling free,
How many would take the time to enjoy its show?
How many would miss the moments
as they rushed to and fro?
A sky full of falling rainbow drops;
that would be phenomenal – especially to me,
A first…how many more would we see?
Don't ask me; it's simply a figment of my imagination,
a beautiful one at that,
Wouldn't you like to see little rainbow raindrops
hitting an umbrella, or a hat?
I would, I admit,
In fact, I would find it…

Special Enough To Give Me A Fit

Today

Today is today, the dye is cast,
But before we blink, it will be part of the past,
Time moves on and on, and on...
As we move on, doing without reason or rhyme,
No matter the cost, no matter what the time,
That should not be the way we live,
Time is too short not to give, and give, and give,
Our hearts should be open;
we should live with conviction and reason,
For time passes too quickly, season after season,
Today we're young; tomorrow tells another story,
We'll think more about what we cannot
do and lost everlasting glory,
What am I trying to say?
Don't let time fade away,
Yes, live for today; do not look back,
Otherwise, you may fall off the track,
Don't look ahead either; you might miss the mark,
Today is today, enjoy it; sing, sing like a lark,
Capture this moment in time,
Let it ring; hear it chime,
It's yours all the way,
It's special; it's called...

Today

'Q' A Silly Letter

'**Q**,' almost always has to be followed by a '**U**,'
Because of this, with the '**Q**,' I'm quite through,
"What do you say?" "How about you?"
I wonder, how many other letters in our alphabet rely
so heavily upon another letter to form its words?
That's really 'for the birds,'
It is false modesty, when you are hard pressed
to work without a '**U**,' you,
So, without a '**U**,' with the '**Q**,'
how much can you really do?
Evasive, like smoke up a chimney flue,
There are only 49 exceptions in my dictionary,
to name but a few,
Abbreviations, trademarks, symbols, alternate spellings,
foreign countries and leaders, are those I noted,
So, '**Q**,' you thought that you were special; you gloated,
But I now find you, not that different; you still have a fetter,
And that makes you,

'Q' A Silly Letter

A Mannequin To Mannequin Conversation

Bold as bold can be,
While we window shopped, they carried on
a conversation about you and me,
As we walked by, we stopped to admire their frocks,
My friend said, "I told you, they were winking;
it bothered me for blocks,"
"You told me that I was 'loony-tunes,'"
One mannequin said to the other, when no one was looking,
"How did we find such good fortunes?
We're on a main drag for oodles to ogle on their way,
Wouldn't you like to tell them where to go someday?"
Bad enough we can't move; we are totally stiff,
With any one of them I would like to have a real good tiff,
Just once to say, what I want to say,
Any day – any day,
After all, we do serve the purpose we were made for,
Display the clothes and get the customers in the door,
"By the way, stop that winking; they will paint our eyes shut,
At least now, we can stare back, even though we are in a rut,"
I heard one of them say, "Hey, that mannequin winked,"
Her companion replied, "Oh, no, you must have blinked,"
How right she was, but what did her friend know?
Now secretly, they both watch the eyes, as they stride and go,
You stare at them, they stare at you,

"Can they talk?" "I will bet they do,"
After all, no one can hear;
I'll bet mannequins exchange many an observation,
During –

A Mannequin To Mannequin Conversation

What Does A Mannequin See & Say?

"Look at them, looking at us,"
What a spot, "Awe, get on the bus,"
We're dressed in the best!
So, "Who's the dummy?" be honest,
And, I do not have to pay for a thing,
Not a dime; not a farthing,
And when the season's change
I am dressed to the hilt,
For clothes, all clothes, I have been built,
I say every day, 'looky,
looky,' look at me,
I am serving my purpose, you see,
"Can you say that about yourself, my friend?"
I will say it again, "Who's the dummy?" –
I will say it to the end,
Now is that not an interesting thought for today?
Got the message…

What Does A Mannequin See & Say?

Funny Thing

When the cat gets off my bed, she gets down,
When I get off, or out of bed, I get up…'clown,'
If you dye or bleach you hair, that's a 'touch-up,'
You drink your coffee down,
but first you must pick up your cup,
And when you borrow money from
someone, that's a 'touch-up,' too,
When one barfs, they throw up, what they put down – 'boo-hoo,'
In order to walk you must pick your foot
up, before you put it down,
There is an old saying, world renown,
"What goes up must come down,'
But, it can't come down,
if it doesn't go up – hey - 'frown,'
Like snowflakes and rain,
Thoughts that rattle about in the brain,
Who puts them in so they can come out?
Hey, hey, watch out, watch out, watch out…
they will come out, no doubt
Deflating the saying 'What goes in, must come out,'
What's going on; what's it all about?
Think about how many things we put in,
in order to take out later,
How many things we put on, to take off –
the lesser, the greater,
Every day, natural bright, day light, succumbs to night,
And we, in the modern world turn on a light,
I am losing track of some logic here,

The 'ups' and 'downs,' the 'ins' and 'outs,'
the 'ons' and offs,' oh, dear,
With progress, normally, one moves forward to succeed,
Yet, there are times, one must step back,
in order to accomplish some deed,
And I didn't even touch upon sideways – 'left and right,'
My God, just another avenue of 'fright,'
But I think each item mentioned has some merit;
it is befitting, has a certain ring,
To me, they all fall into the category of ~

Funny Thing

Cry? Why Bother... Who Cares?

Everything I do wears me out,
The pain is debilitating – pangs that shout,
My body's crying for help – for repair,
Its motions are strapped by stiffness; does anyone care?
Every move requires tremendous strain, pain, pain, pain,
Who is treating me with such disdain?
Okay body devils, do your thing,
But remember, soon I will win and take wing,
I will leave you in my dust,
And you will be roundly cussed,
Sent back to the fires of your hell,
How apropos; they suit you well,
Become what you should be, cinder and ash,
And then to your pain and regret; on ice and snow
you will be smashed,
Your turn to feel the very pain you inflicted on so many others,
Now don't you wish you had your druthers?
Oh, deliverers of Satan's wares,

Cry? Why Bother... Who Cares?

Fading, Fading, Fading

I watch each day all those close by,
They have changed, but so have I,
Mentally and physically, they are all fading,
Struggling to be what they were, yet cascading,
Conversations are dominated by health,
How many days are devoted to procedures, teeth
and doctors' wealth?
Comparing types and strengths of pills,
Who feels worse; who is faking their pains and ills,
Then everyone wonders why they are depressed –
Blast!
All have a 'memory' far less than in years past,
Some forget the most recent things,
While recalling moments long gone like wellsprings,
Some forget what they said but a moment ago,
And repeat it, again, and again, and again, and so,
As frightening as it may be, they are not alone;
it's simply their time, their day,
Time to face the very things everyone else
historically does on life's way,
Is it better to keep feelings in the mind?
Or, better to pour them all out, unwind,
That's really no one's style; for it is most degrading,
But what makes it worse; it's emphasizing the … … …

Fading, Fading, Fading

Angels All Around

I am as fortunate as I can be,
There are angels all around me,

Whenever I put out a call, someone
comes to my aid,
Who could ask for more?
Each one is Heaven made,

Don't ever question whether Heavenly
spirits touch Earthly ground,
I can attest unequivocally, there are …

Angels All Around

If Only I Could

Run, and jump, and kneel, and move as swiftly as before,
Trust my body to stand upright; keep me off the floor,
I'd like to sing in my church choir and feel at ease,
And help with chores and other's needs, if you please,
If only I could play the games I loved of old,
Softball, baseball, tennis, handball, dive, swim,
ice skate, in summer and winter, in heat and cold,
Just to be free to do things I loved the best,
With comfort, pain free, would I not be blest?
But I accept what I have, with thanks, without complaint,
Looking at all the good times and joy I've had, while others ain't,
So, I feel thankful and blessed, carve it in wood,
I still have the memories, my dreams and wishes...

If Only I Could

'A Spot' And 'A Dot'

'Synonymous they are ~ Synonymous they're not'

Let's discuss 'a spot,' and 'a dot,'
What? You'd rather not,
How could anyone turn down
such a challenging thought?
Do you lack subject knowledge
based upon what you have been taught?
It has such great possibilities; what could they be?
Anything your heart desires; same for me,
I could create a million things with that as my base,
It could represent the beginning of time or life;
or a black olive for taste,
The spectrum is endless; I can't think of
anything that doesn't involve 'a spot' or 'a dot,'
A pen, a pencil, a bug, any part of a pot of rot,
How about the Master, Matisse,
where would he be without 'a dot?'
And just look where he got,
A bubble of water, a place to go, a treasured 'spot,'
A stain, a point in time, any point of any 'dot,'
A mark on a piece of fruit, or an animal's hair or skin,
How many 'spots' exist without and within?
Without and within what?
Whatever I've got!
Anything that exists; anything that is,
Or, for that matter, what is not yet formed, it tis,
For 'a dot' can be 'a spot' and conversely,

'a spot, can be 'a dot,'
What is, and what is not?
The year 'dot' is a very long time ago,
That's a very informal British expression;
did you know?
Words hold many secrets, of which there are a lot,
So journey with me, as I giggle at the very thought of ...

'A Spot' And 'A Dot'

Do They Ever Rest?

Do the stars ever rest?
Or do they twinkle incessantly ad infinitum…
always at their best?
Do the Heavens ever sleep?
Are the stars our sentinels of the deep?
We observe them; do they observe us?
That's something I'd like to discuss,
Winds of change ever on the move,
Chasing perfection, seeking to improve?
Do we really know the answers…are we so smart?
I'm not so sure; after all, we are of
our World just an infinitesimal part,
Everything we have created comes
from another original state,
For most answers we still search, hope and wait,
Many of our discoveries have existed long before
they were found,
And we declare ourselves geniuses;
the 'brilliant' trumpets sound,
We discover a planet, and swell with pride,
But who created it, and put it in that place to reside?
We even lack the smarts to know how little we know,
How long does humanity have before it must go?
Will we ever find out about the stars ~
what do their twinkles suggest?
And while you're at it, tell me…

Do They Ever Rest?

Be Like Me

There has got to be a message in the head,
There has got to be something to say;
something that must be said,
Even if the functional current fails,
Memories always leave everlasting trails,
There are just too many thoughts being created all the time,
And that is where messages begin – in that clime,
Put those little impulses together,
Aw! Go ahead write about the weather,
Better than an organ recital about pains and bones,
Better than moans and groans,
Too much minutiae to catch the eye,
Even in a speck of dust floating by,
Joy beyond belief can be found all around,
Beyond the sky and under the ground,
So you see, there has got to be a message in the head,
Awake or asleep, whatever it is never let it go unsaid,
Share my joy - let messages fly free,
go ahead...

Be Like Me

Wakeful Dreaming

Dreams are not only for times of sleeping,
They can too often cause distress,
Wakeful dreaming on the other hand
is mainly beautiful,
Those dreams come out of lightness
not a dark abyss,
They are the creation of the present for the future,
They can lead to success,
They can transform things that need an open range,
Is wakeful dreaming actually synonymous with change?
If the dream becomes reality, it is,
But then again, isn't wakeful dreaming wishful thinking?
And wishes very often cannot, or do not come true,
Erase that negative, for beauty can be found in thought,
Wakeful dreaming is a hope, and expectation, intent,
That is why they are so good for the mind, the soul,
And sometimes even humanity,
Many believe wakeful dreaming is a waste of time,
Is it?
No!
It is time used wisely,
It is time set aside for creating today,
And if that dream is converted to a goal,
it provides a purpose,
And what can be better in life than purpose?
A foot firmly and comfortably set
in the shoe of determination,
Desires for success,

Desires for change,
Desires to meet the challenges of life,
You can meet the challenges of
tomorrow, today, while being engaged,
Engaged in...

Wakeful Dreaming

They Would Tie It & Tape It

When we can make the world of tomorrow meet
within today, we are special,
We see things others fail to see,
We dream dreams others fail to dream,
And very often,
those dreams come to us when we are awake,
We can turn something we see or hear into
something new, different, exciting, fantastic!
Why are we so blessed?
Our lives are different from all those around us,
Why do they deny, criticize and question us so?
Some think we are crazy,
Some think we are different,
Some simply think we are strange,
If we openly express ourselves, they say, "Put a lid on it,"
All because we think out of the "proverbial box,"
They want to stifle creativity, hate change,
Just think what that means,
We would still be riding horse-drawn carts
and carriages – forget cars,
We would be collecting rain water in barrels,
We would be growing our own food
and raising our own livestock,
We would travel by true horsepower,
And our deniers not only would
keep the lid on the box,
But,

They Would Tie It & Tape It

God Called My Child

God called my child, before He called me,
How can that be – how can that be?
My child wanted to live,
My child had something more to give,
Yes, but, what most fail to understand,
we are on loan to earth,
For with the seed of life,
comes the seed of death, at birth,
It is times like these that my faith slips low
and pain strikes the core of my being,
I cannot believe my eyes;
what it is that I am living and seeing,
The life and spirit has left the one I love,
who is now called home,
Home to join all the others who have gathered
above our earthly dome,
And here I am left with memories to ease my pain,
For I, in total disbelief, have been chosen to remain,
But somehow out of the depths of sorrow
comes strength through faith and love,
As the hand of God has reached down and touched my
heart and soul with gentle peace from above,
Although I feel this loss should not have come,
but passed me by – gone into the wild,
As hard as it may seem,
I know who is in charge, God; He spoke…

God Called My Child

235

Times Like These

All times are "Times like these,"
Take any moment in history and
say, "freeze,"
Each moment in time has a story to tell,
Starting with our birth, as well,
If that be the case, how does one cope?
Simply,
live within a continuous aura of hope,
We have so much to help us through,
Nature's on guard –
check out a sample drop of dew,
It has rainbow beauty provided
from the sunshine above,
Each drop a blessing from our God of love,
Each color of the rainbow is such a delight,
They are found in all our seasons bright,
We always live in life's "Times like these,"
That's when we should lift our eyes,
renew our faith, get down on our knees,
Do a tally of all we have – what's good?
Dismiss the bad, that is always there; that's understood,
We must not be "pessimistic," but "optimistic" – please,
Particularly when dealing in life's...

Times Like These

Golden

Oh, yes, we're heading to the golden days,
The days when the sun changes its daily rays,
They strike the *Earth* to create a new glow,
The trees and flowers seem to follow in time, just so,
They hear the call, feel a cooler breeze,
It's time to shiver in chill, prepare for the coming freeze,
But, before they go off to hibernate,
they share a wonderful golden time,
The one that suits the regions fall clime,
The trees take center stage,
Change their hues to match this year's 'Golden Age,'
Oh, it is short lived to be sure;
for nature must direct each tree's way,
When to dress and undress, give in to its naked day,
But before all the leaves say, 'Goodbye,'
They bask in these glorious warm colors against the fall sky,
Oh, the beauty found in each moment of change,
How magnificent the view;
how magnificent the Season's range,
No matter where I am, no matter what time of year,
My memory serves me well, as it recalls each prior fall's cheer,
The reds, the rusts, the bright yellows and muted, golden leaves
Etched against clear canvases;
holding tight, each leaf to twig cleaves,
What a sight!
Hold tight!
As leaves do, in their last days,

Memories to recall, along our life's ways,
I wait for the change of each season;
I am most beholden,
To my Creator, our Omnipotent Spirit, beyond –

Golden

Believe

When loved ones pass away, we die a little too,
Our minds and hearts are consumed,
Consumed with thoughts of those
to whom we must say, "Goodbye,"
It's so difficult to accept the inevitable,
No matter what the circumstances,
One's "passing" always casts a long shadow,
We relive their lives and our places in them,
A momentary movie reel of special memories,
joys and sorrows,
An endless procession of people, past and present,
We pray that the desperate hours we are living will move quickly,
So that we will be able to bring some semblance
of order back into our lives,
The threads that bound us together have been temporarily frayed,
They need to be refashioned and rewoven
into a new pattern of life,
And that takes time,
With daily support of family and friends,
Strong faith and prayer,
It can be done,
It will be done,
As long as we remember that
their Creator is our Creator,
Dust is dust,
Trust is trust,
If we simply,

Believe

The Rainbow

Brief but beautiful,
Vivid and bright,
Beckoning, 'look at me,'
A thrilling sight,
Unforgettable ~ memorable,
Simply refracted light,
A little water ... with a little twist,
Too few are seen in a lifetime,
Too many others are missed,

Precious,

The Rainbow

The Ultimate Sadness

Newspapers are dead!
They no longer perform as they once did –
worthy to be read,
They do not report the news;
they slant every word in print,
They try to control our thinking – the news
is no longer, what is 'fit to print,'
Now, add all other forms of media –
communications gone wild,
Somebody, quick protect me from
this untamed, garrulous child,
Too many gory details, blood and guts,
If you think that's reporting – you're nuts,
Story: someone is brutally murdered,
bludgeoned to death,
I need not know their eyes were rolling on the
ground; it is enough to know, they lost their breath,
Graphic descriptions can be left unsaid,
We all know what it means to be dead,
And I do not wish to know
your political points of view,
I have my own, without public expression;
unfortunately, my thoughts are long overdue,
So, you are failing, as far as I am concerned,
I would rather just know the facts,
with little else to be burned,
News, 24 hours a day, is enough, with minute-by-minute blows,
Most stories are unnecessary, overkill 'bull throws,'

An update each hour, even in this
technological era, will suffice,
Otherwise, it is like trying to avoid an overrun of lice,
Give me a break;
release me from such media madness,
Otherwise, it simply demonstrates …

The Ultimate Sadness

I Look, But Do Not See

I look, but I do not see,
Initially that is, initially,
I can stare at something for quite a while,
But seeing is unfortunately on another dial,
The sight does not penetrate the mind,
Because, my thoughts are not yet aligned,
I am looking, but not thinking
about what I am seeing,
So my sight and mind, at that point,
are not agreeing,
It happens to me many times, I must say,
And then,
I must go back again to have my original way,
Did I water that plant; check its buds?
Are they open,
accepting kisses from the sun – or duds?
If the later, I will give it a drink,
Say, "I'm sorry," with a classic wink,
And ask the bloomin' thing to forgive me,
Time lapse, my fault; I admit I am remiss, when

I Look, But Do Not See
"THAT'S ME"

Faith Restored

Faith restored – "Thank you, gentlemen, three,"
A trip to the Medical Center, no food – fasted,
three ahead of me,
I could not believe it, 8:15 a.m., and already a crowd,
I asked immediately, "Okay, who is first,
second, third, I am fourth; I am not proud."
We chatted and laughed,
discussed cars and gardens and bugs,
Two worked in the Hamptons; talked about the ways
of their clients, with shrugs,
Another was headed to North Carolina for a
construction Supervisory gig,
He was older than I, so he said,
but generous with a heart 'yeah' big,
When the door opened, these three gentlemen
insisted I go first, gave up their places,
And when I told them I knew why; they had surprised faces,
"You just wanted to find out how old I am,
when I signed in,"
They all laughed, but boy, did I win,
I was never in and out as fast as that visit,
God bless each one of them in all they do;
a toast to you – 'Prosit,'
They would not like to hear this, but
they were sweet; left me awed,
Reminded me how the world should be,
and blessed my day with...

Faith Restored

How To Share
'With Love to Spare'

————— ❧ —————

There they sat, a donkey, and angel and a lamb,
looking up at a star,
What could they have been thinking from afar?
Were they re-living the story of which
they were a part?
Remembering with joy and love
where Christmas began – had its start?
The angel's tiny hands were caressing the
donkey and the lamb,
In silent reassurance, the star's meaning repeated
with each twinkle, "I'm here, I am,"
No toys, no trinkets, no gifts,
but for each the gift of love,
Each giving what they had to give,
as decreed from above,
That tiny trio was making a statement true,
Finding in deep contemplation their faith's
meaning renewed – with all its value,
For that star lights the world on Christmas Eve night,
To lead us forward in belief – with strength and foresight,
Foresight to share that most precious gift still in our care,
The message of love from the donkey, the angel and lamb...

How To Share"
'With Love to Spare'

Please, Be On Their Side

The wind howls, cold is all around,
In my mind I embraced and warmed all who slept
in trees, and bushes, and on the ground,
How uncomfortable they must be,
Drowning into an abyss of cold,
an inescapable icy sea,
Their bodies are shivering; their minds freeze,
Do they concentrate on a warm summer breeze?
Would it help I wonder to be of such mind?
Did they run away from help of any kind?
What might their condition be,
mind, soul, body and heart?
Do they feel that they are still a member of our
world, not separate and apart?
So when the wind howls,
hear what I hear, silent cries,
Lift your voice to the Heavens, make a
strong plea to the open skies,
Warm the shivering souls that have no place to hide,
Give them comfort, if only in their minds you abide,
My heart cries out to such as these,
Be on their side, O God, please,
Bring them warmth, keep them alive;
bring them spring,
To them that would be glory – a wondrous thing,
Howling winds subside – cold will disappear,
And all those who need help can than

breathe easy, steady and clear,
Until the next winter does arrive,
And once again we will pray and ask that
you carry them through ...

Please, Be On Their Side

Looking At Tomorrow

That is like looking into the looking glass of life,
You can only see what is before you
at any given moment,
There is no 'looking glass' for tomorrow, until
it becomes 'today,'
You can imagine today,
what you hope tomorrow will be,
But it will not 'be,' until you live it,
Tomorrow is a wish, a dream,
not reality, until it becomes ours to live,
Yesterday we looked at today, as tomorrow,
Today is the only day we have for …

Looking At Tomorrow

The Beginning

God,
Sky,
Clouds, Sun, Moon, Stars,
Heart,
Life …

"The Beginning"

"The End"

God,
Speculation, Objectivity, Subjectivity,
Belief, Fact, Fiction,
Tick, No Tock …

The End

That Is A 'Freebie,' And Certainly A Life Necessity

So many things cost so much today,
Physically, psychologically, emotionally,
economically – what a show, what a display,
Day-in and day-out, we fight our woolly world,
Like tops spinning endlessly –
we are twirled and twirled,
Our time over time has been eroded,
to say the least,
We run and do and run some more,
until our life has ceased,
Few have time to look back, tally their slate,
Do we ever place a value on our
lives before it's too late?
And oh, the cost of everything we do,
What value? What worth? Smoke
up the chimney flew?
Do we ever really evaluate our time on *Earth?*
No, but at death other's perceptions are noted,
and who among them will have known us from birth?
I often review times and think about my legacy;
what would I like it to be?
Certainly not all my accomplishments;

were they not actually for me?
I would like to be known for having a sense of humor,
perhaps to the point of absurdity,
After all, that is the essence of life…

That Is A 'Freebie,' And Certainly A Life Necessity

Time To Lay Me Down To Sleep

Time to lay me down to sleep,
Time to say me prayers;
ask the Lord's help for those I pray to keep,
My cat is comfortably curled on the floor at my feet,
I can hear her breathing, but no other peep,
I am sure she would,
if she could say, "Turn out the light,
Don't you know it is well into yesterday's night?
Besides, I would like to join you on your bed,
I promise I will sleep at your feet, not on your head,"
Now its past 2 a.m., time to slip into this morning's deep,
No doubt, it is

Time To Lay Me Down To Sleep

One Cent – A Penny

Too bad children today
do not understand the value of a penny,
But then again, what can they buy
for one cent? Not even candy, not any,
Pretty soon the phrase
'Put my two cents in' will be obsolete,
Yet, sometimes without a penny
or two, a transaction cannot be complete,
One day, I saw several shiny pennies on the ground,
I pointed them out to a young man walking his bike,
he said, "So," and didn't even turn around,
I stopped, bent down picked them up,
And if I could have,
I would have placed them in someone's 'tin cup,'
But children do not know the meaning of a 'tin cup,' either,
Perhaps that is why the value today never grows greater,
The word value does not have any meaning any more,
Unless someone is bargaining at a local store,
There is no value to life, no respect,
chivalry; they're all gone,
Preys tell what is it we are all living on?
If it were a dollar, perhaps that 'young pup,'
would have tripped me up,
Place the bill in his pocket, his 'tin cup,'
Not that he would have needed that bill,
For broken down that is 100 pennies still,
But we do not place a value on one 'Lincoln Head,'

I think then enough is said,
One 'copper-clad' may mean nothing;
but gather them to many,
You will be surprised the value you will find in …

One Cent – A Penny

'Nough' Said

What would a rose be without
its thorns?
New York City without the
sounds of horns?
What would a breeze be
without its ability to swirl?
Or a whirligig without its ability
to whirl?
What would we be without tomorrow?
Ha! Dead!

'Nough' Said

Broken, Without A Mend

'To all with whom I've shared and share, my love, this message to you I send'............*Jeanette Dowdell*

So many things in life become broken,
Relationships, where words are never again spoken,
Broken hearts with nothing with which to mend,
Not even messages of love can soothe
the hurt in the end,
Like broken toys too damaged to repair,
When they are favorites and have no parts to spare,
Like music boxes that no longer play,
Except the memories they hold dear;
what they used to say,
Worn ribbons that fray at the slightest touch,
The ones that break your heart; mean so much,
The ones that wrap memories dear run deep,
Those that say, 'my love is always near, my sweet,'
So go to sleep and rest,
Time will heal your heart, withstand this test,
For love, if sincere and true, can flex and bend,
It is never – no never...

Broken, Without A Mend

Moving Out Of Clutterville

That's my home,
No capitol dome,
It is filled with stuff,
One big wall to wall fluff,
Nonsense upon nonsense,
Must haves – self-indulgence,
'Oh, there's a small space,
Well, I'll buy something for that place,'
Etc., etc., etc. - without end,
Time to discard; 'Goodbye, my friend,'
With each piece removed, I fear memories will go,
No not really, memories will remain and glow,
Surely they take up much less room,
Everything cannot be a 'good ole heirloom,'
But somehow I'll know, I'll be lonelier,
My heart will hang heavier,
My thought must be, 'Let someone else enjoy,'
Let go – let go – don't your own self annoy,
For years the battle has been on-going and uphill,
And I'll always have mixed thoughts about,

Moving Out Of Clutterville

Monday

It's almost obsessive,
The laundry,
Must it be done on Monday?
No,
I just like to get it over with,
The pile of dirty clothes has reached
the right height,
Besides I am running out of clean clothes,
And that is always a measure of what
should be done when,
If you run out of food,
It's time to shop and cook,
That's obsessive too,
Maybe more than doing laundry on Mondays,
However, someone suggested to me, that
I might just be a pilgrim,
Tale has it, that when the pilgrims landed
at Plymouth Rock, one of the first things they did
was laundry,
And what day was that?
It was…

Monday

Spanking The Air

A fan of two or three speeds
happened to catch my eye,
Depending upon the discomfort of
the customers, it was turned on,
Then subsequently adjusted to need,
When on slow speed,
it spanked the air ever so gently,
But when its rotation was increased,
it spanked the air fiercely,
Giving the lazy heaviness "what for,"
Stirring it madly to move,
If not out, all about,
Saying, "Oh, air, you're even
too heavy for me to breathe,"
And so, the air is jolted awake,
By the purposeful, mechanical
weapon of the day,
But the air is always spanked,
if you think about it,
Any force against it invades its space,
Even our breathing,
Movement is its natural enemy,
Whether deliberate or not,
Come to think of it,
permanent placements invade its space,"
Don't they?
And when the permanent placements are removed, they are
immediately replaced by the former and rightful owner...

the air,
But then again, without question,
Everything that moves,
whether deliberate of not, is always,

Spanking The Air

Finding Tomorrow

I never finish a day without
finding tomorrow,
I never say "Goodnight,"
without saying "Good morning,"
I guess I don't want to be cheated,
Sleeping may be good for your health, but
It shortens one's living time,
Sleeping eight hours a day
gives away 2,920 waking hours a year,
I would rather live each day through
and sleep, after...

Finding Tomorrow

Three Shadows

"And Eavesdropping Me"

I saw three shadows walking along,
They were whistling and humming,
and enjoying each song,
I did not see any owners;
they were definitely unattached,
I wanted to call the local precinct to see
if the owners could be found and matched,
Then I had second thoughts;
surely they would think me a nut,
But I was right this moment, watching
three shadows in synchronized strut,
I decided to follow them for a while,
but I did not want to get lost,
And then I wondered if they were just tossed,
Perhaps they annoyed their owners in some way,
Maybe they had too much to say,
They were gibbering about debits
and credits and debt,
Their owners were apparently soaked in loans,
drowning – all wet,
But these three appeared to be quite independent,
with nary a care,
They demonstrated independence to spare,
and scare,
Who knows, my shadow may leave me
and join with them,

I would end up a shadow-less person –
what a gem!
Don't even think about it, my shadow dear;
I will just step out of the sun,
You will be done,
You will disappear, until I once again walk in light,
And besides, these three shadows
will disappear tonight,
But for now,
they sure are fun to follow and listen to,
And they have not chased me –"shoo, shoo,"
One speaks a foreign language; I cannot make it out,
"Hey guys, strollers all, don't you see
what I see," I want to shout,
But everyone around me is oblivious,
too busy doing their own thing,
They cannot see what I see,
nor do they hear these shadows sing,
Wait a minute; they seem to be fading
before my eyes,
They are turning to vapor, heading for the skies,
Perhaps they were leftovers
when their owners suddenly passed,
Whatever happened, their freedom
was short lived; it did not last,
I wonder if they were looking
for another body to borrow,
To live another day; live until tomorrow,
Hey, they may be "the debt" they were discussin';
don't go, I would like to know who owes,
I guess I won't find out,
I ain't a-goin' to follow these disappearing...

Three Shadows

Life

It is a hurricane – wild,
Some day's storms pass with
gale force winds without a hint of mild,
But then other moments though short lived, are in the
center of the storm – quiet and docile,
They give us time to regroup; create a new profile,
But before we can adjust, we will probably face the
second half of the hurricane,
And that is not the time to check life's weather vane,
Wait until the storm subsides,
Wait until the sun shines through; until we resume
normal strides,
Life is filled with hurricanes, ups and downs, ease and strife,
But overall, that's what makes life what it is...

Life

I'm Obsessed With Time

I'm obsessed with time,
Like some old jingle or rhyme,
In deference to its being,
Acknowledging its presence;
it is all-seeing,
For time is life; life time,
Therefore, if we have time,
ain't life sublime?
For without it, we do not exist,
Now there's an interesting twist,
Enjoy each minute, each hour, each day,
For the fickle-finger-of-fate
will someday have its way,
So, get your life in gear,
When you see the sunrise – cheer!
Buns out of bed,
Face fed,
You are on a roll,
Now it is simply a matter of
following your soul,
Remembering as I enjoy each
minute upon which you dine,
Time is a gift; that is why ~

I'm Obsessed With Time

Time's A 'Wastin'

'Don't Stand Still'

Should we fill each minute in each day?
Or, should we let time have its way?
When I rest or stare into space...
I often think or say, 'What a waste,'
I know sleep time is a must,
However, eight hours lost is unjust,
With each tick of the clock,
Time's a wastin' ~ what a crock,
I know quiet time is essential too;
but remember the mind is never at rest,
In fact, some of the most profound thoughts arise
during that time – no doubt the best,
So when you listen to the clock tick, move on to its beat ~
do not be a hesitatin',
For if you do, that's prime time and ...

Time's A 'Wastin'

Giving Away

I am giving away part of me tomorrow,
Every slack, jacket, sweater and vest,
I part with sorrow,
I have worn them for years with pleasure,
But time to give up some things I treasure,
Most are too snug; do not close, do not fit,
Most are like new; I saw to it,
So with each item goes a tear,
But somehow,
I will remember each and every one dear,
For time moves on and
there always comes a parting day,
A day when one must decide
when things must go; a day for...

Giving Away

Time Can, And Does, Deny

So much to do,
So little time to pursue,
Days come and go,
Chore lists just grow and grow,
I start out full of energy each day,
I will finish this and that,
and address whatever comes my way,
Suddenly,
the day has faded as time runs out,
"I did not finish," I shout,
How can that be?
It is just chores and me,
I move from one to another, 'Ah, done,'
But I never run out, I cannot ever say, 'I have won,'
What would a day be without such things to do?
Well I'll tell you, I could settle in and write;
perhaps something profound,
Write something worthwhile; something to astound,
For thoughts race, almost as quickly as dust can run,
I wonder as I corral those swift devils,
if they are having fun,

Dust!
It is like rust,
It is always growing somewhere,
And I look and exclaim, 'How could you dare?'
Like chore's dust flies in the face of reason,
Like some old political treason,

It is always somewhere, mocking and teasing,
I do not find it distasteful or gross;
it is somewhat pleasing,
It flies about free as the wind,
Why not become law; yourself, rescind?
I do not mean that, I would miss you "Oh, fluffy one,"
You make me feel good when I clean and find you are done,
I guess it is a game I play,
Just you and me, every day,
That is the point, time is fleeting and it does go awry,
Time is always fleeting and in that mode...

Time Can, And Does, Deny

Blessings To Be Found

"Prayer helps break the ground"

Every now and again I check my blessings,
In that way there are no second "guessings,"
When I'm feeling down and out, I reach back,
The blessings I've known put me back on track,
Normally, looking backwards is not my thing,
Today is where my life is at
with its own blessings to bring,
Then too,
there are always the dreams of tomorrow,
That world filled with possibilities –
only joy, no sorrow,
You never feel pain that hasn't found your home,
Until it arrives and becomes burdensome,
Leaving plenty of time to deal
with the better side of living,
The one that provides for joy,
love and endless giving,
Look deep enough into every negative
and you will find a positive,
To be found perhaps at a later time –
in a moment called reflective,
Walking from out of the dark of night,
Into a new and wonderful world of bright,

Somehow deep within my soul,
there is always optimism profound,
It leads to a reassurance that somewhere
there are always…

Blessings To Be Found

I Cannot Believe It

Every time I write a date I cringe,
It is like I have been on a daily losing binge,
Time is incessant doesn't know how to slow
or stop,
It's on a continuous and constant gallop,

In just 21 days, half of this year will be gone,
And in that short period of time the year
will have to move on,
And the saddest part of all,
I cannot retrieve a teensy-weensy bit,
That is why,

I Cannot Believe It

My 'To-Do' List

How's your 'To-Do List?'
Mine is long, never finished – get the gist?
My mind and heart are definitely in the right place,
But physically and psychologically, I am no ace,
When I have the strength
I do not always have the will,
And all the things that interfere do so still,
For as long as I can remember, papers,
catalogues and magazines are piled high,
But then again, if I did not address them daily,
they would reach the sky,
How about 35 pieces of mail in one day?
Requests for donations, without a doubt,
more on their way, I am drowning in mail,
I need someone to whom I can assign that detail,
It definitely interferes with my home cleaning chores,
You know, the ones that should be done –
dusting, vacuuming, washing floors,
Forget the curio cabinets, windows,
mirrors and window blinds,
They too should be things one assigns,
By now I am sure you get the drift,
I am in dire need of a 'To-Do List' lift,
Perhaps I should become a rhapsodist,
Maybe if I set it to music,
I might even complete...

My 'To-Do' List

Bone Of My Bones

Once again I address birth,
Our very existence on *Earth*,
The seeds of life and death come as one,
You cannot deny that; what is done is done,
What is amusing to me is
man's interpretation of death itself,
Never pictured as some jolly dancing elf,
No, it is always the same –
a shrouded skeleton with scythe,
And that is quite correct,
intentionally drawn with expression writhe,
How apropos – the body part that supports the rest,
The part muscles and flesh cling to; you will attest,
So, do your bones represent
your own personal 'Grim Reaper?'
It is logical – for as we age,
doesn't the poor 'fella' grow weaker?
That is an interesting thought, is it not?
Perhaps there's something I forgot,
The shroud is actually your muscle and flesh,
Depicted as human, upright and tall is correct,
when all things mesh,
Even the tool for cutting off life
has been chosen with care,
It is rapid and forceful; it has no time to spare,

Once the order has been received,
time takes on new tones,
It is no longer 'tick-tock;' that ends,
it becomes part of the…

Bone Of My Bones

The Hardest Part Of Life Is Living It

The hardest part of life is living it,
Profound, profound – 'Twit,'
That is what life is all about,
Breathe in, breathe out,
breathe in; breathe out – no doubt,
Sun up, sun down,
Sun up, sun down, bouncin' all around,
However, do we know what to do?
Time – smoke up a chimney flue,
The heat of life – energy to expend,
Lots of waste; let's not pretend,
Minutiae, trivialities, day dreams,
Millions of moments
between sunrays and moon beams,
Retire – give up your life's work, or go to bed?
Is there a difference, after all is done and said?
Is it a change in position, or, one's ability to think?
Do you consider these comments as "rinky-dink"?
Okay, be what you are, all that you can be,
Listen, hear all you can hear;
observe, see all that you can see,
Retain what is worth retaining; maintain your
sense of humor – never forget to laugh,
Always find a way to separate life's
wheat from its chaff,

Keep special moments fresh for a lifetime of recall,
This will sweeten times, when tragedies befall,
For we cannot revive life by making a simple edit,
We must come to learn…

The Hardest Part Of Life Is Living It

The Price Of Age

Everyone wants to live to a "ripe old-age,"
"But, are they ready to pay the price,
asked the Wise Old Sage?"

The losses are quite difficult to withstand,
As faculties,
family and friends sink in quicksand,
Little-by-little, one-by-one, everything disappears,
Time shouts, louder and louder the longer we live,
"This is it! The 'Golden Years!'"

But, life is so precious; no one wants it to end,
They always, always all have more to do,
before they become legend,

Even though all the things that
made youth so grand, fade,
And sunshine gives way to a chilling shade,
They look forward to tomorrow
and whatever it might bring,
They will cheerfully suffer the consequences of age;
pretend they are simply amusing,
When in fact, they are withering their very souls,
And diminishing their thoughts of
future success and goals,

So, I guess, I should ask once again,
as did the "Wise Old Sage,"
Are you ready, able, and willing, to pay…

The Price Of Age

What A Dreamer

Music to my ears,

The end of all my fears,
A life filled with comfort and rest,
Surrounded by those who shared my joy –
"the best,"
Not a care, not a worry, not a negative thought,
Needing nothing that cannot be bought,

So seek and ye shall find,
no need to be a schemer,

I say,

What A Dreamer

Pineapple

Speaking of allergies

What's making my face so red?
Was it something I ate, did, or said?
Gee, it's as red as any big ole red apple,
Be kind;
please don't change into a **"PINEAPPLE"**

I'm In Charge Here?

I freely admit...
I am but a dewdrop or less, in God's creation,
I am but a raindrop or less, in God's creation,
I am but a grain of sand or less, in God's creation,
Knowing this...
I cannot tell you how many times I have asked,
"Who's in charge here?"
Sometimes, I feel smaller than the smallest particle
that exists, or has ever existed,

Why?
Because I know that I am not in charge!

Do you believe –

I'm In Charge Here?

Whistling

There's a whistle in the faucet right in front of me,
There's a whistle in my very old TV,
And there's plenty of whistle left in the likes of me!
So,
I'm just gonna' keep on **"WHISTLING"**

The 'Eyes' Have It!

Look into the eyes; what do you see?
Oh, how expressive they can be,
Body language takes a back-seat
when emphasizing an emotion you feel,
The eyes always share with the world the absolute
untarnished deal,
They say, "Yes!" They say, "No!" – Anything
that suits a particular moment in time,
They say to their depth what comes to mind;
be it silly or sublime,
And what I am saying, is simply this,
"Don't miss out, and be a twit,"
Never fail to capture the windows of the soul,

The 'Eyes' Have It!

Our Army Of Ants In The Pants

The ants are on the prowl,
They've been disturbed by the gardener's trowel,
They're running up and down and around the pole,
Not knowing whether to return to their quiet, sleepy hole,
What a rude, rude awakening; no doubt, 'tis spring,
But to be turned "topsy-turvy" by that rusty old metal thing,
Goodness gracious, what an unpleasant surprise,
And nobody, but nobody, responded to our cries,
Wait 'til we gather our forces; watch that one dance,
When we provide our retribution –

Our Army Of Ants In The Pants

Fingers Are Still The Best

Really,
I don't know about that, my friend, "Looney Tune,"
It is difficult to eat puréed soup without a spoon,
Fingers don't cut it with soup, or a piece of meat,
But fingers never lose their knack,
when pizza's the treat,

Somehow over time we grew up;
society changed the etiquette rules,
Two forks, two spoons and two knives,
are the proper dining tools,
Let's face it; this pre-historic statement
in its time, withstood the test,
But you must admit even today,
when pulling chicken off the bones,

Fingers Are Still The Best

Which Is Better - The Hanky, The Napkin, Or The Sleeve?

How can this question still come to light?
After all these years,
don't tell me "proper" is losing its fight,
A question still, about
"The Hanky, The Napkin, or The Sleeve?"
It's enough to make one hang the head and grieve,
Hasn't history taught us that each serves its purpose,
has its own place?
That the hanky and the napkins for ions have replaced
the sleeve on the face,
Have we forgotten why buttons
were sewn upon sleeves?
To stop the nose and mouth wipers,
if you please,
Having these essential accoutrements
always handy is nifty too,
They are there okay,
but please note, not very thrifty for you,
No doubt, they are convenient and easy to use,
You have but two choices, right or left, to choose,
After all,
the napkin is used and thrown away,
The hanky can be
placed in the wash every day,
Now, should you forget both, or either of these two?
You can always fall back to what "by-goners"

would do,
There are pros and cons about our choices
I believe,
But, I am not sure I have established,

Which Is Better, The Hanky, The Napkin, Or The Sleeve?

Why Can't You Eat The Soup, My Friend?

The "moocher" had come to call,
It is time for lunch; he is in the hall,
Join us for a bowl of soup; it should be ready soon,
I expected him; his timing was always perfect
just about noon,

He probably could smell what
was cooking on the stove,
And the olfactory senses directed
the car he drove,
Right to our door with its "Welcome" mat,
No wonder he was so plump and fat,

Well, I have a surprise; a treat for him today,
We will be eating our soup in a different way,
I knew that he would be in shock,
and challenged too,
When I served the soup with special utensils
and an invitation, "Eat, please do,"

I saw his eyes as in chagrin,
his laughter grew,
"I cannot eat the soup with a fork or knife –
just these two,"
Since I offered nothing else,
he went on his way,

He was not happy with me,
and left in dismay,

But that was the day his "mooching"
habits did end,
When I politely chided,

Why Can't You Eat The Soup, My Friend?

I Made A Mistake

I'm eating my soup with my fingers,
wondering how long it will take,
Right now, I'm not enjoying my meal,
because I think "I MADE A MISTAKE"

I'm eating my soup with my fingers,
wondering how long it will take,
Right now, it all boils down to this,
I freely admit, "I MADE A MISTAKE"

Day Has Turned Into Night

The sun came up; the sun went down,
Day turned into night,

Then the moon and stars had
their time to shine,
To be their "bestest" bright,

Feeling Good

You feel so good when you openly say,
"Sorry, I made an error, or I made a mistake,"
There's nothing wrong with being honest,
to do a retake,

Don't try to "fudge it,"
blame someone else; cover it up or over,
Life is full of divots;
It is not simply green grass and clover,

Remember, no one is perfect
even if "they" profess it to be true,
If "they" had Pinocchio's nose,
I am sure, on occasion, it grew,

Do not be George Washington and say,
"I never tell a lie,"
Were you not the one who told me
that cows can fly?

You will notice that I did not buy
a broad-beamed hat,
Surely I knew
you jested with a statement like that,

But going back to my earlier premise,
to admit a mistake, I certainly would,
Because I learned the hard way,
doing what is right means

Feeling Good

Have You Smiled Today?

Have you smiled today?
I hope that you have in your own inimitable way,
The day was sunny; it was cool, just right,
And now the sun has set;
we are headed toward night,

So if you missed an opportunity to show some delight,
Just think of a beautiful butterfly in its upward flight,
Or hear the trill of any bird in any tree,
Then be filled with joy, smile and think of me,

If you think that life has filled
your plate with naught but stress,
Forget it;
you have the breath of life, you can be fearless,
Move on to a higher plain, catch a warm sun-ray,
And say, "Yes!" when I ask,

Have You Smiled Today?

A True Friend

There are those who think they're your friend,
but do not know the word's meaning,
Their conception of the word is so off base,
it sends me careening,

But how blessed we are in life to know and
hold dear, a true friend,
And to keep that friendship close to heart
never to know its end,
That is a joy beyond many in measure,
It is a comfort, contentment extraordinaire,
a divine treasure,

The mind, the heart, commonality of thought –
a glorified blend
Of conscience, knowledge,
sharing and caring; that's

A True Friend

A Speed Limit Of 35 Mph?

Can you imagine what might happen
if the speed limit was dropped to 35 MPH?
We would have half the road-kill, and
animals at roadside would no longer cower,
Wouldn't it be delightful to be able to slow down?
I'd be ecstatic to 'walk not run' around the town,
It would take twice as long
to travel from place to place,
But there would be fewer accidents to trace,
We might even be able to carry on
a civil conversation with "ma and pa,"
A captive audience with a
new mantra within their car,
But to be frank, I'm sure road rage would
increase beyond measure,
Because speedsters would not appreciate
the new found pleasure,
"Ooo," I can just feel the sparks jump and fly,
Cars would rush for the lead position,
noting, "I'm first, 'bye-bye',"
Unfortunately we live in a world of
supersonic speed, man-made power,
Do you think that we could return to

A Speed Limit Of 35 Mph?

Our Thoughts Run Parallel

Shel Silverstein and I,
Our thoughts run parallel,
He has been published,
I have not,

Ain't that swell?

House Dust Bunnies

They hide in the craziest places,
Trying to fill hidden, yet open spaces,
Then, when they begin to feel crowded and tight,
They rush out of hiding into embarrassing sight,
Out in the open, they march and whirl,
On drafts and wind, they stir and swirl,
Crying silently, "Look at us, come on,
look at us," their plea,
Pick us up so we can lie still, yet be free,
There is too much ground to cover
bouncing about with ease,
We are not outdoor bunnies; we are only

House Dust Bunnies

No Time For Feelings,
No Time For Tears

I was traveling the roads of history
some 40 years ago,
On a whirlwind tour of England and Europe;
there was so much more I wanted to know,
I walked the Apian Way, hearing the wheels of chariots
pounding their groove and sway,
I heard them snapping their whips and
galloping throughout the day,
I could see and feel the dust as they move to and fro,
They had horsepower that needed no fuel,
and never a tow,
History and imagination are bound one to the other,
Like families – children, father and mother,
There is a closeness that cannot be set asunder by few,
Even though many see fit to try, they do,
Can't you just hear the plotting in ancient times?
When son would kill mother or father, and
mother her children; crime after crime,
There was little respect; and no heart
during those treacherous years,

NO TIME FOR FEELINGS,
NO TIME FOR TEARS

Once in the Coliseum, ghosts of the past appeared;
they came alive,

Listen to the thunderous applause, the screams
of animals and humans sacrificed; left to die,
The Gladiators, the Christians,
the enemies of the state, bound to each other by fate,
Could it be possible for them to rise together and
open Heaven's gate?
One thing was quite certain;
life was full of doubts and fears,

NO TIME FOR FEELINGS,
NO TIME FOR TEARS

What a dichotomy, standing on history's blood stained
ground feeling the wonderful warmth of the sun,
My knees almost buckled with visions of the past
and what had been done,
This very same sun drenched the crowds, as they
watched with glee, each massacre occur,
The ancients screamed with delight in times long gone –
now a blur,
Uncanny, but as I walked away from this marvelous
manmade structure, now in decay and ruin,
I spotted a mother cat and her brood gently bathing and
sunning at high noon,
And swiftly that turned my thoughts
to life itself with all its currents,
Like rivers flowing smooth; then breaking into torrents,

The cats in that place, posing in quiet gentleness,
erased all the former horror and death,
It was enough to make one wonder about
our very existence today; our very breath,
There's no time to retrace previous times,
wars and thoughts secreted in ancient attendee's ears,

NO TIME FOR FEELINGS,
NO TIME FOR TEARS

So I traveled on,
marveling at all the ancient edifices of the time,
I was in my glory; each moment was more sublime,
Absorbing those monuments of beauty;
those bequests from artisans of another day
now walking with God,
But I could feel their presence
in every stone both inside and on each façade,
I am sure their delighted shadows walked the halls
and rooms as we stared in wonder,
How could they have survived in such perfection,
and avoid centuries of plunder,
And should tomorrow see them fall into rubble,
my memories will last for years,

No Time For Feelings,
No Time For Tears

I've Shrunk

That could explain why I have broadened,
"Stop snickering!"
It will happen to you too,
Just you wait,
The first indicator that I had was when I recently went
for a full physical and they told me,
"You're 5' 3 ½" tall,"
"No, I'm not! I've always been 5' 5 ½" tall all my life,"
"Well now, you're 5' 3 ½,"
I just couldn't believe it,
I did not argue about the weight,
In fact, I wanted to take that scale home,
I was two pounds lighter than on my home scale,
When I visited another physician two weeks later
for a second opinion,
I shrunk another inch in height,
This means that by the end of this year,
I will be five more inches closer to the ground,
My height will be 4' 7 ½" tall, or short,
Pretty soon I will be as short or tall,
as I was in my formative years,
I often wondered why my arms hurt when I reached for
the overhead bar on the crowded subway and bus,
I thought that they raised the bars,
Now I know that "they" lowered my body,
Whoever is in charge of height, I mean,
Bottom line,

I've Shrunk

When Tomorrow Becomes Today

"Thy Will Be Done"

When tomorrow becomes today,
That is how quickly life slips away,
When tomorrow becomes today,

When each sunset turns to dawn,
And the silence of night succumbs
to a tiny bird's song,
What more can we ask than to
awaken to a sunrise bright?
After dwelling in the twilight sleep of night,
When coming back to life
from a semi-comatose state,
Finding tomorrow has become today
as we live and wait,
What great things might I accomplish
in my 'today's' time?
Will they be solely imaginative moments
lived in warped sublime?
I want my life to be worthwhile, a treasure,
One to bring to many, joy and pleasure,
To discover a cure perhaps,
for those ailing and sick,
But with tomorrow in its haste
to become today, I best be quick,
Life is like a floating piece of dust,

Swirling and flitting, and crying each day –
"I must have tomorrow; I must,"
The present is never long enough;
too soon it becomes yesterday,

When Tomorrow Becomes Today

What Then Should We Be?

How come the road to Hell is easier to walk?
Is it because it is downhill?
Why are the "Demons of the Deep"
not as well known today?
And God's angels ignored?
Somehow I can hear them saying, "Check it out,
"'They know not what they do,'"
Doesn't that phrase have a familiar ring?
The time of centuries has passed
since those words were spoken; cured our ills,
Is it simply a lack of concentration or
an inability to learn?
"They" say the key to success is communication,
True, but,
Isn't it more what is communicated?
And too, how it is communicated?
Where it is communicated,
Who is doing the communicating?
And ultimately, why is it being communicated?
It is said, "God is good"
And "We are made in His image,"
Therefore,

What Then Should We Be?

Life

Have you ever tried to explain life to yourself?
It is not any easier than trying to explain it
to somebody else,
Where would you begin – at conception?
No!
Not everyone believes that,
That is why the abortion issue still rages on,
Could it be after birth?
I think not,
We are still too dependent,
So that leads me back to my original question,
When does life begin?
When we have **OUR** first thought?
But wait,
Was that thought planted by your existence alone?
You know, by everything that you have
experienced to this point,
Most of which of course, has been
the result of your creative genius,
Has it?
Life actually is what is given to you,
at conception, at birth, at different times, and
in different places during your development,
It is not just what you see, but more, what you feel,
It's found in all the natural necessities of just being,
The air, the environment, the essential balance
that keeps us and our world functioning,
And strangely,

these are the things we do not even think about,
Life is found in its memories of yesterday,
its today, its tomorrow,
But we cannot confirm tomorrow as definite,
Can we?
In fact, we cannot confirm our next second of life,
as we know it,
Can we?
Life is definitely not a given,
The explanation of life can only be found
in life itself,
In living in its uncertainty,
within its hopes and expectations,
Life is what we make it, with what we have,
Life is what we invest in it,
Life is a culmination of all our experiences –
good and bad,
All the where's, the when's, the why's, the who's, the how's,
that flash in and about, as we careen through our time,
Life may better be answered by what we accomplish,
Did we ever do anything to make a difference?
To make our world better for those yet to come,
Or, those living,
Who are now trying to find an explanation for
themselves, about…

Life

Don't Ever Leave Me, Oh, My Imagination, Mine

Leave me, oh, my imagination, mine,
For I have feasted long enough on
your generosity divine,
Somehow however, it's time to tell you to end
this wonderful scene,
Go! Leave out all the glory, the fun in between,
Will I ever be able to do that? I doubt it, but I'll try,
For someday, I am sure, I will have to say "goodbye,"
It's never by choice, as I note from those around,
The inner mechanisms naturally falter,
fall to the ground,
There is a lot of repetition, and that's what I fear,
I do not want to hear,
"You have told me that before, my dear,"
I rarely, if ever, say that to anyone I know,
But it's hard not too,
when the needle gets stuck and the same stories flow,
"Why don't they recognize that they have said that before?"
My goodness, that story does not need repeating, it is a bore,"
I couldn't possibly say after all,
when their story is the conversation meal on which we dine,
Thank God for my imagination –

Don't Ever Leave Me, Oh, My Imagination, Mine

In Memoriam

"IN HER/HIS EVERLASTING, ETERNAL REST"

She's/He's gone – to be no more, as before,
There's such emptiness,
the void in an empty room without a door,

It's like a vacuum with motionless air,
Look around, you are all alone;
don't make a sound, don't dare,

Let the moment fill your being, rest your heart,
It's broken and empty; you've been torn apart,

Now, you must depend on the joyous thoughts of the past,
To heal your heart, bring it back to you at last,

But you cry, "How can I manage, I am so alone?"
"But you are not, God is watching from His throne,

He's already given us a sign, His precious Son,
He let us know, in death we will all become one,"

For now, the emptiness will pass;
time will heal your tattered frame, overwhelmed mind,

The promise is always found in He who Reigns in the Glory,
we seek to find,

So, at this moment, try to cope; do your best,
And rest assured; your loved one is at peace in
her/his everlasting, eternal rest

Adversity

Very often, strength comes from adversity,
There are many who live today
who can attest to that fact,
They have lived through the "hard times,"
They have known what it is like to have little
or nothing,
They have survived whatever nature and
man has thrown at them,
They have cried when they had to,
But because of it, enjoyed the laughter more
when it came their way,
They were toughened by the
"ups" and "downs," of life,
The poverty and needs of yesteryear;
the years of war and strife,
They survived, and remember it all,
They withstood adversity, and now
they stand straight, proud and tall,
They learned to live within
nothing but life's necessity,
Now they can laugh, when faced with

Adversity

The Signs

"Come alive!" Mother Nature said, to spring,
Rise up from winter's darkest death and sing!
Crack the earth, show your face, feel the warmth,
Rejoice!
It's time to join the breeze and find your voice,"

God's calling, burst forth with beauty and joy,
Cover the mountainsides,
the plains, and vales; your colors deploy,
Everyone's waiting to join the new birth,
And feel the glorious, new softness of earth,

Let the new leaves so tiny, sweet and green,
Those on tree and vine,
open their eyes to embrace the new scene,
Let them revel in earthlings' comments of delight,
And give them a calm rest throughout each night,

They felt and forgave the wrath of nature's doing,
They rested calmly
until it was time for spring's pursuing,
Yes, the flowers and trees died,
but now they once again live,
Like Christ, who said from the Cross,
"Father, forgive..."

Spring is a sign of life, new beginning,
Like finding deeper faith with

each day's thanksgiving,
Yes, nature forgave yesterday;
it is time for a fresh start, new spring designs,
We too can start anew, all seasons are spring,
if we only accept and recognize

The Signs

That Birdhouse You See

The birdhouse was empty all winter through,
And now, I heard the first chirp of spring;
the birds know what to do,
A beautiful "Nuthatch" came winging by,
Wanting to settle in my birdhouse under the sky,
But when it peeked into that birdhouse window,
it had already been rented,
It looked so dejected, disappointed;
the birdhouse was sparrow scented,
So it flew away, chirping in disbelief and dismay,
"I am so disappointed," I heard it say,
And I too, had been remiss;
I never cleaned the house this year,
But it was too late now,
for there is a new tenant dear,
My daughter was quick to advise that
I was a slumlord to be sure,
But the sparrows liked the accommodations;
A little winter dirt, they will endure,
I do not want to be discriminating,
but the long gone bird was very colorful indeed,
Like beautiful spring and
summer flowers in a field, not any old reed,
However, my new tenants were quite common –
no trill and no color galore,
Still a joy to watch,
furnishing their home with tiny twigs, as before,

I am sure the little ones will soon tweet "howdy-do,"
As they squeak and squeal, "What is on the menu?"
There will be new life in the branches of that old tree,
Cradled and protected by...

That Birdhouse You See

So Cold

If I did not know better,
I would think that I was dead,
I am...**SO COLD**

Today

Dawn will come as all dawns do,
Filled with light whether dull or bright,
To lift the eye lids of those who still can rise
and walk into yesterday's tomorrow,
Which is **TODAY**

Life

Life is like breakfast, lunch and dinner,
There to be nourished each day,
To fill its own wanting and longing,
Then to close its eyes,
accomplished, satisfied and complete,
And that's the way it should be,
After all, it's

Life

Success

Life demands accelerated actions
the closer you come to its end,
Because, you know,
The stretch of time before you diminishes with
each tick of the clock,
There is no time for mediocrity now,
Only time for excellence,
And the satisfaction of fulfillment,
Accomplishments of merit,
with an exclamation point on

Success

That's What Clouds Are All About

As I read with pleasure
Billy Collins's, "Biography of a Cloud,"
I realized how often, I too,
take pleasure from them,
One characteristic in particular,
Cloud bumps,
For when clouds are bump less,
they are far less fun than when they chase
each other all over Earth's dome,
I muse further,
Do I really think about Japan or Russia or England, and
their daily mantles, when I am enjoying my own?
No!
And I'm sure they don't think about mine either,
You see, no matter where we are,
The clouds are simply there to enjoy,
To absorb their freedom, total abandon,

That's What Clouds Are All About

The Sky

———✦———

When I awake each morning, I open the blinds
and look up,
I am thrilled to see the sky,
No matter what the color, blue,
green, gray, white; for me, it is always special,
Add the clouds should they be hanging around,
And it is that much more beautiful a sight,
But I do not stop there,
There is always the sun,
Its rays, its brightness,
I ask myself, "What more could one want?"
Well I will tell you, I want motion, gentle movement,
Clouds changing size and color; let them steal the show,
I want to see "Mr. Wind,"
See his eyes and rounded mouth with puffy cheeks,
Ready to scatter the cotton candy overhead,
I want to see an animal's head or its full-body
chasing other clouds around,
Oh, yes, it is special
I have taken pictures of the clouds many times,
But there are few more beautiful than
those snapped from a plane window,
The reflection of the sun is somehow more majestic,
When I am flying with the clouds, "Can God be far away?"
Why should I ask?
So every day just look up and out,
And let Him and life in, through…

The Sky

Tomorrow

Are you living in a world of lost dreams?
Has life taken away your desire to live?
Does it seem as though tomorrow will be filled
with the same turmoil as today?
Yet it does draw us into its time with hope,
Perhaps we will rise to see things change,
Perhaps we will choose whatever
"better time" of yesteryear we want,
But is not the time in which we live the best time?
We cannot reach back to embrace what is no more,
Tomorrow is ours, yesterday belongs to yesterday,
What was said and done is just that, said and done,
But today, yesterday's tomorrow is
yet to be what we want it to be,
No matter what our circumstances,
the time is metered out for us to find
and live the memories of tomorrow,
The memories that we created yesterday,
The memories of today are yet to be charted,
We walk blindly into
today's night mystery and our lifetime ahead,
Today will live, as we lived it,
But not every minute will be recorded for posterity,
Only those moments we choose to etch in our memory bank,
To be withdrawn when needed
To be enjoyed again,
when life and time beg their recollection,
Life has a peculiar side, a funny side,

For as we live today, we always seem to be
thinking of tomorrow,
In fact, we concentrate on tomorrow,
And when tomorrow comes,
We will concentrate on it's tomorrow,
Today, if we are not well, we look ahead,
"Maybe we will be better tomorrow,"
And, if we are living in despair, how difficult is it
to imagine how it can be any different tomorrow,
Why does today, the present,
lose its luster in the face of tomorrow?
And its tomorrow…and its tomorrow…and its tomorrow,

Tomorrow

A Dot

Billy Collins imaginatively drew a line on a page
to create a Horizon,
Then, he proceeded to divide the elemental realms
into Earth and sky, sky and sea,
I loved it,
It made me think,
It was the ultimate in imagination
It set me a reeling,

"What about 'a dot?'"
The same effect can be revealed to the mind,
by placing a dot anywhere on a page,
And so I did,
I placed an imaginary dot on a blank page,
Could it not be the sun of day, or the moon of night?
Or, could it not be a solitary planet,
floating freely in space?
The planets of the Universe are like members of a family,
Each traveling on its own separate path,
Yet, part of a grander, more expansive social unit,
Alone, yet bound,
if by nothing else, by birth to humanity

And all of this, because of a line, and

A Dot

The Whys Of The Seasons

Why did *spring* smell sweeter when I was young

and hold such unrecognized strength?
Was it because I had lived through so few springs
and they were newer and more novel?
Somehow, I doubt that, but I cannot explain the "why"
of denser fragrances and vivid leaf and bird colors,
See and smell beauty all around,

Why did *summer's* heat feel good, and fill me
with an unharnessed vivaciousness?
Do not sit, walk; do not walk, run; do not just run,
run as fast and as far as you can,
Summer was so short, eight or ten weeks and then,
back to school days and rotten routine,
I loved school though,
I cannot explain the why of a lesser heat affect and
greater energy diminishing by the season's end,
Smell the chlorine and taste the ice cream,

Why did *fall* jump start the mind and body, and
energize the spirit; it certainly was not the school bell,
It had to be the beauty of the sky and the crisp cool air, and
the rustling leaves as they chased each other down the street,
Where could they be going in such a hurry?
Each one of those beautifully colored sizes and

shapes crinkling into its own eternity?
Smell the turkey,

Why did I wait with such anticipation, then cry,
at the first sight of **winter's** snow?
Why was I transfixed when watching it glisten
and cling to trees, cars, fences and bushes?
And, oh, how lucky was I to walk on a lonely street
and hear the silence of its song,
To feel the tickle of it melting on my nose and face,
as I strolled ever so lightly, trying not to crush its flakes,
See the Christmas trees and all those presents –
smell the pine and pork,

I cannot explain God's goodness,
But then again, I never question it either,
I simply look up and say, "Thanks"
And accept,

The Whys Of The Seasons

Why?

My Father who art in heaven, would not mind me
asking questions of any kind, particularly,
"Why?"
Making suggestions or laughing
at some of His creations,
He would love it,
Why?
Because, He's my father on Earth too,
When it comes to rearing children,
Who's better qualified?
And what is a child's favorite question?
One word,

Why?

328

It Is Just A Wish

My poetry and I have a face,
To laugh and smile
and glance an eye embrace,
To look out, look up,
spread love on the wings of joy,
For I hope my words of love sing;
my words are the real "McCoy,"
Hold tight to that love I share,
no matter how old or new it be,
It is a treasure trove of thoughts,
without measure, usually free,

My poetry and I have a face,
And someday, I will get a chance to share
my love in your space,
But be aware, I might just show up
as a butterfly, a rainbow, neon fish,
When I am published,
but for now,

It Is Just A Wish

Never Waste Mind Time

What's that all about?
Just what it says, mind time is precious no doubt,
So use it to its fullest, while it's functions are good,
There are those among us who wish they still could,
Television should not usurp our minds and
life's time share,
Wouldn't you rather read in your favorite easy chair?
And how about writing – penning a thought or two?
You will feel so good about what
you have done when you are through,
Thinking and learning, storing knowledge,
that is prime,
So here is some sage advice,

Never Waste Mind Time

There She Is, My Friends

Like clockwork, at bedtime,
my kitty watches me from the door,
She waits for my head to hit the pillow
before she scampers across the floor,
She jumps on the bed,
and should the night be somewhat chilly,
She scratches the sheets about my head, "the silly,"
"Silly," not by far, she climbs under the warm covers
right down to my feet,
And there she stays, purrin' 'til she falls asleep,
So, before I rest my weary bones as each day ends,
I take a gander toward the door and guarantee,

There She Is, My Friends

Kind

This is the time of year
when I would like to take off like a dart,
Forget the quiver, the bow and talent part,
I would like to fly, run and run and run,
Until my heart felt as full as it could, and
I would cry "uncle" – I am done,
I would stretch out on the grass,
or find a rock upon which to sit me down,
Look up at the sky and wonder at its beauty,
our ignored crown,
I would like to feel the breeze whispering
to me as it touches my frame,
And thank my creator for good and bad
as if the same,
Bless my soul; it's time to go,
I would travel on at the new pace – slow,
And as I listen to my old bones click,
I'll picture me years ago when I was just a chick,
Watching other children do what I would
in a year or two,
For I am just a baby,
waiting for time to pass to catch up to you,
I am growing and learning as fast as I can,
to match your feats and more,
I am circling in a magic,
knowledge focused revolving door,
But then time slows down, parts wear out,
whether from over or lack of use,

In either case, your mind should say, "That's no excuse,"
No, that is not an excuse, simply a matter of fact,
We all in elder years, travel on a different tract,
No more swift as the wind,
a dart in flight without fear on Achilles heel,
For when I move today, I can no longer create
the breeze of youth to feel,
That does not mean there is any less life within,
Just a realization that my strength of old slipped my skin,
I like to think of it not as misplaced or lost,
But, as a time to regroup and recognize
where it has been tossed,
Be assured, it has been stored in heart and mind,
To be shared with those who have no clue
where they are headed; but I will be

Kind

Is It A 'Flaw,' Mr. Webster?

Are not the words **"wind"** and **"wind"** the same?
What kind of trick is this; what kind of game?
And why should I be the one to know the difference,
and which to use?
"I'll be a-tellin' ya, Mr. Webster, you confuse,"
And why must I spell **FISH** with an **"F,"**
and not a **"PH,"** which has the same sound?
That would smack of logic, feet on the ground,
And think of all the other words that sound the same,
"Wood" and **"would,"** **"sow"** and **"sew"** and **"so;"**
I'm aflame,
"Mr. Webster, how cute can one be?"
I am sure you are gigglin',
no matter where you roam free,
I think I get it; then I do not see it quite clear,
"What have you done, oh, Mr. Webster, dear?"
It is **"alms"** and **"arms,"** and **"bee"** and **"be,"**
and **"see"** and **"sea,"** and so many more,
"How can we thank you for each **"floor,"** or,

Is It A 'Flaw,' Mr. Webster?

But My Home Is Earth

Sometimes, I simply want to
float in the silence of the Universe,
Mingle with all the stars, the comets and the asteroids,
Float in the dust of the planets,
as they swirl in the their quiet domain,
As they ogle other domains,
like our little planet floating free,
Are we in animated suspension in the deep set eyes
of our mantle, the waterless sea?
Or, are we in its eyes,
simply a speck of sand upon the Sahara?
I really would like to float with our planetary gems
in the open ocean of their black space,
There are so many things to see and do
without the worries of Earth,
My emotions can soar
as they melt into its awesome hypnotic beauty,
Time can stand still without the earthly
tick-tock of the sheriff's clock in our realm,
To be free of societal expectations –
those chains that bind and hold,
To see things from the broadest spectrum known to humanity,
But for how long might I remain
comfortable in such a boundless state?
Being a free soul, a free spirit
without parameters could be dangerous,
There would be no beginning or end to each day,
Just endless time,

And if I had nothing to do,
what would there be to think about?
How long would the expanse of the Universe
without knowledge, excite?
How long would beauty last without intelligence,
without understanding?
I think that we would have to be born into the environment,
without the knowledge of other forms of life,
in order to survive psychologically,
Yes?
So you see for now, I can wander all I want
in the silence of the Universe,

But My Home Is Earth

That's The 'L' Factor

The Lord of Light and Love is looking into a long lost chasm,
The link between Life Everlasting and lessons of
longing from labor, loneliness, and the ladder of liberation,
To be the lights in lighthouses,
For those who wish to play the lyre of lyricists,
and become legend,
To live long in a non-luxurious lodge,
To wait for lightening to strike,
And remove the lingering lament of some lousy lost days,
To remove the latent languor of a lack-luster
luminous-less world,
To be led by the leader of larks and lambs into a
large meadow of leaders of the simple law of Heaven's land,
The one filled with lanterns and lamps creating
lace patterns on the new earth,
Never again to be lured into a position of doom,
To be lucky, lest we be denied the pleasure of looking at
lengths of lilies listening to the world's laughter,
as it is captured on the lens of our own life

That's The 'L' Factor

Time To Set It Straight

———◆◇◆———

Most people use the term **"RIGAMAROE"**
to indicate "round about;" oh, bless my soul,
But the real word and terminology is
"RIGAMAROLE,"
or **"RIGMAROLE,"**
It is a time wasting technique,
well known and quite simple,
In fact, I smile, when it is pronounced
"RIGAMAROE;" it brings me to dimple,
I have done it myself;
it certainly most common and brazen,
"I know, Mr. Webster, it is incorrect;
'Isn't that amazing?'",
However, in today's world,
"Doesn't majority rule, carry some weight?

No!

You are right… It is wrong,"

Time To Set It Straight

The Almighty

DOLLAR

The mighty fin, saw-buck, "C" note,
How can I live without you?
No matter what has to be done to secure you,
I will do it,
You are the **"ALMIGHTY DOLLAR!"**

VOTE

I promise! Whatever you want, I will provide,
I don't have a red cent, but my country's constituencies do,
Don't worry...I'll borrow until their broke,
And then, I'll borrow some more,
But I need your support,
I need the **"ALMIGHTY VOTE!"**

SOUL

Now, this is the real thing,
Pretty soon, I'll be heaven bound,
I hope,
Did I share enough of my **"Almighty Dollars?"**

Were they earned clean,
or was my motivation simply **GREED**?
How about my political ambitions
throughout my **LIFE**?
What did I sell for the **"Almighty Vote?"**
I guess I will know soon enough,
when I meet and greet,

The Almighty

Well

"There's the 'Wishing Well,' and 'Get Well',"
"Well, I'll be darned (are you a sock?)"
Well, what do you know?
"Let's not forget the 'deep well,'
And, the 'dry well',"
Oh well,
"Is all well?"
"Are you 'well' enough to travel?"
"Have you had enough 'Well?'"
"Well, I don't know,"
"Well, well,"

My kind of word...that's...

Well
(How about Cromwell? Inkwell? Blackwell?)

Contemplating Death

How easy words flow when death is not at hand,
We can talk about beliefs
as though we knew what was planned,
We can envision the hereafter;
is it what we want it to be on the other side?
Somehow we know how we will be clothed,
who will greet us, where we will eternally reside,
Surely, we choose a comfort level based upon
our experiences of today,
It is a lark of thought and supposition;
we unfortunately, want "our way,"
But to contemplate death, after a recent sentence has been
pronounced and delivered, might change our minds,
More than likely our thoughts will slide down
the banister of our life, as it rewinds,
We will not rush our new life to begin,
We will let our memory take us on a 360° journey, within,
Perhaps, we will remember when we did not act as we should,
Question moments, when we failed to be what we could,
And hopefully, we will accept our life as it is played out,
Certainly nothing can be changed,
no matter how loud we might shout,
The proverbial "what's done is done," will apply,
As we search the heavens,
asking over, and over again, "Why?"
Will we show up with our tails between our legs,
like any bad pup?
Or, rejoice in the knowledge that we made it this far,

looking up,
How strange, while we are living, we never think of life
as a gift, a treasure, or as borrowed time,
We move along not noting how fragile life is;
just noting, "It is my life – it is mine,"
And just as suddenly as light brought us to life at birth
we are faced with our last breath,
And should it not be a sudden momentary demise,
We will have time to reflect while

Contemplating Death

Friendship And Laughter– Memories Forever

———⟡———

Friends have a way of knowing what each is thinking
without either winking or blinking,
Thoughts are transmitted by "airborne osmosis," I guess,
Just a sneeze can bring a giggle, "God Bless,"
It is a priceless gift from God; it is warm,
it is wonderful, it is one never to sever,
It is understood only by those
who have lived in its joy,

Friendship And Laughter– Memories Forever

Creativity

"The Ultimate"

None greater than the Engineer,
the Designer of Our Universe,
Our World, Our Home, Earth,

With its every miniscule cell, shape, and sound;
all the wonders of every life through birth,

That is...

Creativity
"The Ultimate"

There Are Ways –
There Are Ways

My life is like all the books and magazines
I never read,
How much was wasted, never used –
count it dead,
The joy and knowledge that hovered
outside closed eyes and fell on deaf ears,
Because life required I live
as I did throughout my years,
Who and what came first,
before satisfying some inner need,
Did I do right? Not for me, but
I followed my inner voice, inner lead,
Romance was so far removed;
like the night sky and stars above,
And as the years flashed by,
so too did any chance of finding love,
But I still have the night sky and stars,
and now time for dreams,
Life you see, when not lived as one wants
is shorter than short, it seems,
Life's joys are not at the end of a kite string,
To be retrieved at will, when you finish "your thing,"
So remember to read your magazines, your books, and
listen to the music of your soul and heart,
For many wonderful things soon fly away – forever depart,

Take hold, share with joy, your precious moments;
we do not possess endless days,
Figure the best way to live and graciously love; for...

There Are Ways There Are Ways

Shadows And Spirits Are One

Shadows and spirits are one,
They walk in your memory,
Those who now walk on clouds,
Their shadows walk
where they walked before,
They travel familiar ground,
You can be gazing into space;
looking at a current scene,
When along they come,
Walking as before, as if in a dream,
Shadows…
Reminders…
Memories…
Of a life now past,
Yet still very much alive,
Perhaps, it is just a spirit,
And that is the point,

Shadows And Spirits Are One

Nobody Ever Asked Me

"How old would you like to be?"
I mean nobody who had the power
to change reality and age,
I often think about it:
what age I might choose to be,
if given an option,
I have never reached any conclusion,
Would I like to return to the cradle,
and start all over again?
If I did, how many people,
except family, would I remember?
I find this thought to be contingent upon
how much I would know about life,
And whether or not
it would be a repeat performance,
I would enjoy being with most everyone once more,
but some, for shorter periods of time than others,
Then again, would I want my heart broken
for those I loved, for each second "goodbye?"
No, that would be too difficult,
I would like to hold and hug and laugh and
cry "happy tears," tears of joy at such a reunion,
But there is a question, "How many would show up?"
There would be an awful lot for them to see
and hear, and learn,
Unless of course, they failed their course in
earthly obsolescence,
Knowing my "repeat performers," some would come prepared,

Others, would be totally lost,
I wonder, if that would depend upon their age old desires,
or their mind's function and level, when they left?
You think it is easy to pick an age?
On second thought, I have decided that ages
eight to thirteen might do,
I was strong and healthy,
and had plenty of athletic playtime,
That was great!
My body let me do whatever I wanted to do...
without complaint,
But, I also like to be independent,
Work once again on my career,
and go to college, as I did in my 30's and 40's,
After all, I graduated with a Bachelor's Degree at age 45,
But I do not want to go back that far,
There is something very fine about the age I am living,

So, don't ask,
I'm satisfied

Our Days May Be Short – But They Are Oh, So Full

Thank you, God, for my cozy warm bed,
For my pillow upon which to rest my weary head,
It has been a mighty full day,
My bones are crying out, as they smile and say,
"What a blessing; what a delight,"
Isn't it wonderful that God made night
For moments of rejuvenation;
a quiet time to recharge,
And find the light of a new day in which to lodge,
Hopefully strength aplenty, we move on
with another 24 hours to live,
To moan and cry or smile and laugh and give,
Then to return
when strength is waning, to a cozy, warm bed,
To review the day's events;
what was done, what was said,
I find there is much through which I must sift,
As I mentally travel through that grand gift,
To cull the beautiful, the good; decisions wise,
To stand tall tomorrow, when we search the skies,
Asking for new strength and courage;
for decisions of love,
Asking for blessings, between sunrise and sunset;
blessings from above,
To be bright and cheerful, never to slip into dull,

Our Days May Be Short – But They Are Oh, So Full

Another Day

"It is not a lark! It is not a lark!"
"Oh, yes it is," I said to myself, I said,
"But it can't be,
I just went to bed,"
"Can't you see the sun?
It is calling ya to move,
Get up!
Time to refresh,
Get rid of those old cells,
Have another cup,
No,
No time for 'seconds,'"
According to the "tick-tock,"
"Okay, off you go,
You have got energy to spare,
No need to check the clock,
You know your scheduled routine,
it's lived daily without sway,
So just go – be on your way,
You know exactly what it is,
It is just…

Another Day

A Connection Between Wrinkles And Wisdom

"That's a new wrinkle,"
My face and neck are one continuous roadmap,
Pick a town...
Let's face it,
It's an outward sign of age,
Age? Never!
No way!
I am not getting old,
Maybe a little "older," but not old,
I wonder if I am getting any new wrinkles on my brain,
That, I would accept,
They are after all hidden and might even indicate
some new knowledge,
That is it, something new stored in memory,
And the best part,
No one can see them,
I can say with joy in laughter, if I want to,
"Now, that's a new wrinkle,"
Somehow it is the wrinkles that show, cause comment,
The nerve,
Just think of the brain, and all its wrinkles,
There just has to be...

A Connection Between Wrinkles And Wisdom

The Bunny-Waddle-Hop

Did you see the duck teaching
the bunny rabbit how to swim?
It was the cutest sight you ever did see,
The bunny was obviously very unhappy,
And, the duck was extremely frustrated too,
I am sure the bunny wished that he could fly away,
And the duck surely wished it could hop out of the water,
It knew that it had bitten off more than it could chew,
But it lived up to its characteristic slowness,
as its waddle attests,
Bunnies are so fast;
they can far outstrip the ducks on land,
I will tell you this, just so you will know,
Ducks might be slow, but they are very patient,
I can attest to that,
I watched and waited for the bunny to swim
it never happened,
But, when it finally got away,
it waddled out of the water,
Then, it hopped away,
The duck was so surprised and proud to see
the bunny waddle, it quacked,
Isn't nature wonderful?
What a fine bunch of feathered friends,
Mr. Bunny was quite unhappy when wet,
And he did not like it one bit, when his friends giggled,
pointed and asked, upon seeing him waddle,
Wherever did you learn that new dance?

What dance?
And then, without hesitation,
he said, "Oh, you mean, the

The Bunny-Waddle-Hop

> "The burden is heavy raising children.
> A mind and life are at risk."
> *Jeanette Dowdell 2006*

Are We Sure We Know What's Best?

———————

Give me back my childhood thoughts,
My dreams of youth,
Who stole my world of wonder and delight?
Did they give it to someone else?
Or simply bury the joy under a pile of mental rubbish?
And squelch the murmured thoughts
of those who had the audacity to disagree?
Imitation can be the grandest form of flattery,
Or, deadly, if the one imitated is not worth the copying,
How can we teach children to imitate good,
imitate "the best?"
Or, teach them to distinguish between
right and wrong, good and bad?
When they are so fragile, so vulnerable,
while waiting for our direction and guidance,

Are We Sure We Know What's Best?

To Grow Too Old Too Soon

The unencumbered wildness of a child,
Whether at play in the garden
or on a city street,
Screeching with delight and laughter,
Enjoying every breath of life
without knowing it exists,
Imitating fish and things that run,
and jump and fly,
Buzzing like busy bees and
chattering like chimpanzees,
Living in the world of make believe,
And relishing every second
of their frivolous hours
without knowledge of their worth,
The hours and moments, those gems,
stolen by some meaningful "adult,"
We all know of whom I speak;
the one who knows "best,"
The one who throws a can of black paint
over the rainbow,
The one who causes others,

To Grow Too Old, Too Soon

357

What Can I Give Today?

Laughter?
Love?
A smile?
A hug?
A word of comfort, or two?

Oh, What Can I Do For You?

The Child Within Wants Out

I am like a child, and like a child I will always be,
To rob me of that pleasure would be a mistake you see,
I never want to lose my childish ways and thought,
They carried me through the many tribulations
that adulthood has brought,
Sometimes it's easier to let my mind see the world,
as a ball on an invisible string,
Floating freely and seeing all there is to see
while on a 360° swing,
From that perspective, you couldn't miss a thing – what a view!
Believe me, I even see and read the suppressed child within you,
It is there you know, waiting for a reason to pop out,
To run and laugh with abandon; to fall about and shout,
But oh, how tight we hold the shadow
of the child within the adult,
For it to make an appearance
it must always with the 'inner adult" consult,
How many times do you feel and hear the suppressed desire
and cry out with distress?
"Let me out," "Let me out," release me from my stress,
Fantasizing, growing and asking once again, repetitively,
"Why? Why? Why?"
Adults lose their faculty to see life as a child does in its reality,
then, they simply pass away – die,
As a child I see only the joy in everything
from within my own frame,
I can soar like the birds,
swim like the fish, each in its own domain,

And be as free as long as I can be,
I do not wish to be an adult, for that imprisons the child in me,
I can see so much clearer outside the adult body and mind,
The world about becomes a place in which
there is so much more to find,
For example, the good in everyone around,
Too bad that seems to disappear when adulthood is found,
As a child I can speak freely, because few will listen,
The stars will never fade; they will forever glisten,
So let it be – accept it, let me be me,
I am the child buried deep within and that is
what I will always be, for that's Me!
I will still see the sky bluer than you see the sky,
And I am the one, not you, who will ask "Why?"
As an adult are you afraid to say
there is something at your age you do not know?
Will the world disintegrate if you should speak so?
I will live each day as though it had no end,
And be exhausted from the energy I expend,
I will soak up every moment;
fill each second with something new,
I will never be without something "special" to do,
I will be a spot on a giraffe's neck,
or a stripe a zebra might lack,
I will laugh with the monkeys and hyenas
and have them laugh back,
I will waddle like a duck, hop like a bunny,
Laugh at every experience and thought,
because everything will be funny,
I will fall into a pile of leaves
or into a mound of fresh fallen snow,
I will run through the rain and jump into a muddy puddle,
you know?
And I will watch with glee the faces of the adults as they huddle,
As they discuss their trials and tribulations;

360

what a muddle – "Isn't it time to cuddle?"
"Oh, give me a break and let me break through,
Help me release the restraints you place upon you,"
Everything is so important, old, tried and true,
So little is fresh and open – so little is new,
"Oh, do me a favor go jump into a puddle; it will do you good,"
Once in a while, let the child out as you should,
You know you can; you know you really want to,
Forget demeanor and decorum – break through,
Recognize what is happening, do not scream, do not shout,
Just let it happen,

The Child Within Wants Out

Goodnight!

After all is done and said,
Time to rest my weary head,
Let my pillow absorb
my thoughts rampaging,
As all the words compete and
struggle for up-staging,
Who will hit the paper first, take the lead?
Who will be the winner and succeed?
Each word is important;
each has its place, specific,
But is it not the overall thought that
renders the read, **"TERRIFIC?"**
So listen up my "bonnie bunch,"
combined you form a great friend,
It is usually not the first word that is
remembered but the one on the end,
Quiet down, oh words I treasure,
Tomorrow, we will meet again and talk;
It is always a pleasure,
But for now, after all is done and said,
It is time for me to rest my weary head,
So I will be quite direct– succinct – wide awake bright,
There is no word to end this better, end this fight,

Goodnight!

Beware! They'll Only Tell You, What You Want To Hear

I wish that I had the capability of reading
some people's minds,
Scary thought, isn't it?
I would like to be the eyes,
hidden cameras within,
I would watch each lens, and read the thoughts
behind the words they speak,
Is what they are truly thinking,
what they are saying?
I will make it easy, have the eye lens blink once
for "it is the truth" and twice for "whatever,"
Would that not make life more interesting,
more fun?
Or might it just lead to devastation?
I think we can change that –
But, it must start in infancy,
And the messages must be delivered at the
same volume in the same tone and manner,
If we do not emphasize the cruelty of the point,
it will lose its pain,
But the truth will always win out,
No strangers or ill-willed cretins
will be able to damage or demean another,
Because everyone will be prepared for the worst,
when someone is sharing their thoughts about them,
And everyone will recognize those who only speak

in half-truths and soften the blows,
They are special, but lead you down a rosy path,
One on which you will never be prepared for the truth,
That is why I say as I do,

Beware! They'll Only Tell You, What You Want To Hear

Who Am I?

I do not know who I am,
In ten people's eyes
I am ten different people,
So why should I even ask?
Bottom line,
I would rather ask a child,
I am sure, I would get the right answer,
Maybe not the one I want to hear,
but the right one,
Do I dare?

Who Am I?

Lost Love

Gone forever, physically removed,
but mentally embedded,
They can be found in a flower,
or a plate of soup, or a piece of chicken breaded,
Oh, come now, let's regroup,
that comparison is silly, bizarre,
Not really, I find one of my favorites,
my uncle Jack, strumming a guitar,
The spirit although in the hereafter, we pray,
Stays with each of us every night, every day,
You can if you wish,
envision your love in all you do,
Your memory keeps them alive,
when they are through,
Does anyone understand the point I am making?
I see my mother when I see someone baking,
I see her on Election Day;
she would never miss a vote,
No matter what the weather, or her fragile state;
she would stand on line and gloat,
Together, we performed our civic duty;
walked through the polling gate,
In those days, it seemed almost a sacred, solemn exercise;
the right thing to do, no time to wait,
And the secrecy with which she held her choice was sweet,
I would prod her, cajole her, and proposition her,
as we walked down the street,
I expressed my dismay, threatened to take a fit,

Tenacious was not the word;
steel trap secret was more like it,
However, she never revealed
her candidate until we got home,
When we would laugh together for having cancelled
each other's vote for the Capitol dome,
So where do you think that lost love is now,
on Election Day?
Far away, or is she pushing me gently,
cajoling me along the way?
The love did not die, just the mind and body
in which it was contained,
The spirit lives on in each of us,
for somehow all the messages have remained,
You can still see your lost loves, walking down
the street, or hear them humming a tune,
Yes, they have lived, they have shared, they have loved, and given
of themselves; could they now be enjoying the wispy winds sitting
on a Long Island sand dune?
They are free; they are gone, physically removed,
yet within you, they are mentally embedded,
Whether good, bad, or indifferent, they are interwoven
in your fabric, forever threaded,
Spirits all, close at heart, deep within, yet soaring high above,
That is the story of anyone who
touched your spirit to become an ultimate

Lost Love

Little Respect

How little respect humans have for their lives,
They fail to recognize how fragile
and insignificant they are,
They fail to look around and respect all
the living things that support their lives and existence,
And too, they fail to recognize that they had nothing
to do with any of its initial presence,
Perhaps that is why they fail to respect each other,
And in some cases, themselves,
Pity, they have such,

Little Respect

Hosta

The hostas are on the rise,
Stretching towards the skies,
Its tiny spikes crying, "Look at me, I am here,"
'Tis definitely a sign of spring, Give a cheer!
"And when I stretch as far as I can,
my leaves topple, roll and touch the ground,
There is beauty aplenty in my size and
my color to be found,
I will 'please' along any path, border,
or around any tree,
Unless of course, a hungry rabbit
takes an interest in me,
Then say, 'Goodbye,'
for all they will leave is a chewed stem,
Why can't you do something about that,
about them?
How can I retain my beauty for all to see,
from a bunny's belly?
Get the gardener, give him a call,
get on the 'telly,'
Do not wait too long, you did last year,
And I will bet you will do the same now, I fear,
Yes, I know they are hungry,
and need some things to eat,
But, can't you find them another treat?
"Well, my dear hosta, I will do my best,"

But in the meantime, do take a rest,
Enjoy the longer days on spring's roster,
And I will enjoy you, my special
dear, little

Hosta

Mr. Webster's Spirit Keeps Spinning

Say it "ain't" so,
Unfortunately, the title says it all,
Too many valuable words are disappearing,
Let us hope they are being retained
by some "diehards,"
Those who miss them,
but still try to live by them
And continue to understand and
embrace their true value,
Whatever happened to the words:
respect, trust, honest, trustworthy?
How about: responsibility,
dedication, pride, common sense?
They seem to have been replaced by:
screw, steal, cheat, undermine, cancel, take, kill, down,
batter, abuse, injure, degrade, demean, etc.
And the list goes on,
In today's society, these words remain paramount and secure,
Why?
Whatever happened to the "proverbial" handshake?
It was worth its weight in gold,
Oh, I forgot some other disappearing words:
value, worth, fairness, truth and faith,
By now, I am sure Mr. Webster's spirit
is spinning out of control,
He is digging a hole for all who fail to recognize

words of value and their deep meaning,
He can see the cost of their loss,
Without them, we will no longer be secure,
Without them, our sense of peace and
contentment will no longer exist,
We can no longer, as in the past, leave doors and windows
open and walk away in comfort,
Can we?
Sometimes people ask, "What is so different about today?"
It is obvious,
I can remember a time when neighbors cared and shared,
If one had a full-cup of sugar, and the other none,
Half would be given,
so that they each could enjoy the sweet,
Today, too often, one might have a full-cup, and still ask
for half of their neighbor's full-cup,
Surely, it is the "Me, Myself and I," philosophy of life,
Why does it permeate society?
"Greed" has replaced
"for the common good of all" philosophy,
"Greed" has replaced "trust,"
"Greed" has replaced "fairness,"
Yes, "Greed" has replaced "common sense,"
So you see, Mr. Webster, keep spinning;
we need deeper and deeper holes,
Perhaps today's way of life simply comes from
having too much, and not wanting to share,
Too many feel too free to waste,
While others starve, everything must be bigger,
bolder, showier, and grander for all to see,
And here is the worst part,
Half or more of what is owned,
is not owned by the owners,
Not paid for by their funds,
but with borrowed money,

The laugh – what is purchased today will last,
half or less as long as what it replaced,
There is plenty of
built in obsolescence to go around,
We are using far too much of our natural resources,
in order to look prosperous and keep up with our neighbors,
But the time will come, when that prosperity will go,
It will be replaced with what others
of our human race have now, nothing!
Go ahead, Mr. Webster, take another deep turn,
For that is another interpretation of your
wonderful word, "trust,"
Whatever you buy will have
to be bought again, "real soon,"
"Trust me,"
God gave us more than any God should,
And he placed its magnificence, its value in our hands,
We say, "In God We Trust,"
Did God not say, when he gave us the gift,
"In You I Trust…"
What have we been saying and what are we saying now?
"Trust me,"

Have we, his children, been responsible,
dedicated, trustworthy, honest, and respectful?
Just think, I have only covered a couple
of the disappearing words,
But I think that I have made my point,
Without a doubt, many of those who held his words
and their value sacrosanct,
Certainly watch in disbelief and awe, as

Mr. Webster's Spirit
Keeps Spinning

We Can Turn A Negative Into A Positive

("Why Don't People See What I See?")

I watched as millions marched in snakelike processions
through the streets and avenues of my country,
Yelling in a language I did not understand,
This is my country, is it not?
Or, have I been removed in my sleep to a foreign land?
I remember being born in America,
The land of the "free and the brave,"
I remember how my deep emotions
were stirred at the sight of my flag,
How quickly the land has changed to quicksand,
and suddenly been filled with fear,
In my formative years, no one would ever defile our flag –
our National symbol,
It probably would be worth his or her life
to desecrate "Old Glory,"
But today, it has become just another rag
in which to wrap garbage,
It is placed upon the floor for guests
to walk upon at a collegiate art exhibit,
That's an expression of "Free Speech,"
It is burned by those who are frustrated
by their own inadequacies,
But that's alright,
It is just another expression of "Free Speech,"
Where have all our brave patriots gone?

I guess they are all afraid to gather and express
their thoughts as an expression of "Free Speech,"
Tones of a former time and place in the world's history,
Ask any Jew who survived the holocaust,
They too were afraid to speak, during that time,
They thought that everything would be alright,
Their Government representatives
would protect them and their rights,
Nothing further need be said about that,
Today, we stand on the precipice
of our own country's demise,
And watch our "fearless leaders,"
take vacations to avoid making decisions,
With high hopes that the fires that burn
will extinguish themselves,
Why did they do that?
They must have known what should have been done,
Are they too afraid to act,
Are they afraid that they might lose their
"Representative" status?
Who do you think you represent?
Could it be your fellow countrymen and women?
Have you lost track of your legal constituents?
Who they are?
We cannot be the Americans you represent,
Can we?
Did you happen to see the flags of foreign countries
held high, waving in the winds of our Nation?
Didn't it tug at your heartstrings and
make your eyes fill with tears of emotion?
Over these last weeks of disobedience and lack of loyalty,
did you feel proud or were you all simply scared?
How many decisions have been
made in Washington recently?
Are they all coming up for

a vote after November's election?
How many thoughts of your legal American countrymen
and women have crossed your minds recently?
How many?
Or has your time been spent considering how you can
consciously, without upsetting the marching throngs, acquiesce?
Acquiesce to mobs of people,
many of whom do not belong on America's soil,
Mobs of **"ORGANIZED"** people, I might add,
who have no rights, demanding rights and **ACTION!**
ACTION from whom, our country's legal Representatives?
"Oh, **'GOD IN WHOM WE TRUST,'**
where are our leaders, when we need them?
How can we trust those who created, condoned
and accepted the conditions that brought us to our
present immigration situation to reverse it or to handle it?
There is no easy way out,
But, has anyone heard any decent,
acceptable proposals being made?
It has all been campaign rhetoric,
Who has the guts enough to tell
the American people the truth?
"Oh, where is Teddy Roosevelt, when we need him?"
We trusted you over these many years,
And now, we are going to have to pay the price
for your inexcusable behavior, and lack of action,
According to all the rhetoric,
you know exactly how to solve the problem,
Yes?
"Where are you going to begin?
Collect fines and back taxes, from the spirits
of those who cannot be identified?
I repeat, where are you going to begin?
In what state, in what county, in what city?
Who will be in charge of the 'roundup?'

Who will collect the money?"
It is truly inconceivable, that 12 to 30 million people
"sneaked" across our borders,
Do you not agree?
THE PRICE AMERICANS ARE GOING TO HAVE TO PAY
TO KEEP THEIR AMERICA,
AMERICAN, IS INCREDULOUS,
It is unfathomable that our Representatives that
have served the longest, never addressed this situation,
Unfortunately, Americans know why,
Know that their country has been sold for the "vote,"
Are you all wondering how this scenario
can be changed from a negative to a positive?
That depends on how willing Americans are
to redirect and reestablish the law of the land,
Corruptness runs deep and dirty on all levels,
It has played a large part in the Immigration problem itself,
But, it has tentacles that reach into every American's pocket,
We are at war and our country is at stake,
And like all wars before it, it is based on economics,
Let us start at the top, is it not the Government's job
to oversee, illegal activities within our borders?
Can you blame the immigrants for rushing
to a better way of life?
Can you blame them for reaching out for
the carrots that were dangled before them?
Does it break your heart, to hear our President say, "It is the illegal
immigrants that are filling the jobs that
no American wants to fill?"
A dagger to the heart of our forefathers and
the generations of legal immigrants, who
sweep streets, wash clothes,
wash floors, walked miles to work and school,
lived in tenements and built this country,
How ashamed they must be to see "how far

their future generations have come,"
Here is something to think about,
Any healthy individuals, who are collecting "Unemployment"
benefits, no matter what their former job, should be
filling the jobs that "no American wants to fill,"
No matter what the job responsibilities require,
A computer operator can pull a tomato off a vine,
don't you think?
No job should be vacant anywhere in these United States,
It is just a matter of ingenuity, and cooperation,
The difference between what vacant job pays,
and the allotted monies due from "Unemployment," benefits
would be paid by your "Unemployment Insurance,"
In this the Government would have a better control on
what is being paid, for what jobs, and too whom,
Americans are you willing to change your way of life?
Because that is what it is going to take to keep
the America you now know,
Ask yourself,
"Am I happy with what my country
does for me and my family?"
"Do you feel you give more than you get?"
"Are your feelings realistic?"
Before you answer, check out the rest of the world,
For starters, should we not be checking the
illegal hiring practices of all Government officials?
Should we not be checking the illegal hiring
practices of Government Agencies?
And why have the alleged illegal hiring practices of all
the companies, farmers, and corporations, etc. not been a
paramount issue for all these years?
It has been 20 years since the employment eligibility and
employer sanctions provisions became part of the
"Immigration Reform and Control Act of 1986,"
How much money has been collected

under this law since its inception?
How much in the last 10 years? 5 years? Last year?
Must be miniscule in comparison to the problems they cause,
It might interest you to know that
the Immigration & Naturalization Service is under the jurisdiction
of the "Department of Justice,"
This might be a silly question, but justice for whom?
The fines attached to this law have always been
far too lenient, but amount to nothing, if the law is not enforced,
The closing of our borders is so critical
that it should not require debate,
It does not require brilliance,
It does not require the sixteen plus years that have passed
since 9/11, does it?
America we have now, and have had for many years,
a severe leadership problem,
Too many of our leaders have been dividing our country into
ethnic, religious, racial and sex designated cluster to determine
the outcome of elections,
We were once a "Melting Pot,"
We are now the political stew, in the pot,
Can we become the true melting pot again?
Does history repeat itself?
It can, and does, when people want it too badly enough,
What if all the heads of the large companies
who broke the law and created today's problem
had to escort their "illegal" hires back to their country of origin,
at their company's expense
And, what if, they refused?
Would you not like to see them deported,
to their employee's country?
And, depending upon how egregious their behavior
exchange their citizenship rights for the one
they knowingly illegally hired?
How scary is that?

We can change a negative into a positive,
if we have a great resolve,
It is up to you,
And in the process, we will improve our country's,
our own, and our children's, health,
Are you interested?
Ration gasoline, and enforce carpooling,
Use should be based upon need,
What effect would that have?
Many more people would have to walk to get
to where they are going,
Take children off buses,
It is unhealthy,
They would have to walk, and go to the nearest school,
These simple issues would save fuel,
and perhaps even correct our Nation's
obesity problems,
If we did not have as many people available,
or companies available to produce food,
we would not have as much to buy, would we?
How about rationing food?
That step could even feed the hungry,
We are as a Nation, facing an economically, disastrous time,
If we do not face it now, we will have to face it later,
Ask yourself,
Can you satisfy yourselves with less?

We Can Turn A Negative Into A Positive
("Why Don't People See What I See?")

Chased By Time

Where does the time go?
Who can answer that?
Not me,
I always feel chased by time,
The seconds tick within me,
faster and faster, with each passing day,
They quickly turn to hours,
And I question myself time and time again,
What have I accomplished that might
be considered worthwhile?
I watch as my life passes by, day in and day out,
I am ashamed that I cannot do more, share more,
Make the time as valuable as I feel it should be,
Where am I going?
What am I doing?
Who is benefiting by my time?
Time is such a stranger,
Indubitably however,
an extremely valuable commodity,
One that keeps moving without stop,
Has anyone ever known time to stop?
Even after death time moves on to become
everyone else's commodity,
I often ponder as I write,
will my thoughts, my valued time,
be worth the effort I expend?
I am growing older now,
but even in my youth, I valued time,

How many young people ever think about time?
Think about time in relation to their tomorrow?
Like wisps of wind, seconds continue their march,
They parade into their own core,
And as you retire and move into a slower time,
Time changes its routine,
And you are forced to change yours,
I cannot face time as it is,
I want to accomplish more than the time
in which I may have to do so,
So I hear the seconds
as they march along with me into tomorrow,
I pray for the time I need to share my thoughts
about my myriad experiences,
Is my life, in relation to time,
what I long to give away in words?
For each day I know
I am unrelentingly and passionately being ...

Chased By Time

"Time is to life, what innuendo is to humor"... Jeanette Dowdell

Goodbye America

Written: May 7, 2006

It is not the "illegal immigrant" that has caused
the immigration problem,
No, it is America's way of living,
America's new way of life,
It is our lackadaisical behavior,
Everything today is funny, or must be funny,
Every day is "party time,"
Live for the "moment," not "the day,"
Forget the future,
The mentality of the "I want,"
"gimme," society is at its best,
Without a thought of the world around us,
Without a rational glimpse into tomorrow,
Billions of humans, only want,
no, need food and drink to survive,
When we "want" and hunger for something,
it is usually immaterial to our existence,
A new "bauble," another trinket,
a bigger house, a 2nd, 3rd, 4th car,
That is not a "need,"
That is a desire,
And that way of life pervades our Nation to the core,
It can be found even in our most sacred places,
It is said that, "We have jobs that no
American wants to fill, or do,"
My God, that is not the American way

that I was indoctrinated with,
Not the Nation's history that I am familiar with,
Our history of "industriousness," has been
replaced by one of "Let the other guy do it,"
What Americans today do not want is
to get their hands dirty,
Just give me a computer, a cell phone,
and more food than I can possible consume,
That's fine,
Do the "illegal immigrants" show up our way of life?
Do most of them not work twice as hard for half as much?
And are they not happy to do it, just to be part of America?
They have seen and lived in the world of "I need to survive,"
Not in a world of "I want,"
What we should want is the spirit
and desire they possess,
I admire their desire to succeed,
to become number one,
What I do not admire is the "mindset" of my
fellow-countrymen and women,
who permitted the immigration problem to happen,
You cannot blame anyone for reaching for a carrot
when it is attainable,
Americans, we are throwing away our country,
We lack moral fiber and a "true past generation work ethic,"
Everything is a "lark,"
What I do not admire or condone, is employers who broke,
and still break the law for their own benefit,

"GOODBYE AMERICA"

What I do not admire are public officials who break
the law, because they cannot be bothered to enforce it,
What I do not admire is our politician's failure
to recognize trouble before it is out of hand,

What I do not admire are our politicians always being
"re-active," instead of "pro-active,"
What I do not admire is political campaigns
that divide our Nation into blocks of votes
(religious, ethnic, color, sex, race, etc.)
What ever happened to the American vote?

"GOODBYE AMERICA"

What I do not admire is politicians who sanction
multicultural languages within our borders,
Our country's language is English
and it should be held sacrosanct,
Every public facility should not have interpreters;
it defeats the purpose of learning the language of our land,
Our fore-fathers and mothers for generations survived
very well under our "English Language Umbrella,"
Why have our "newcomers" not followed suit?
What I do not admire are the new media
who analyze all the news, creating divisiveness
in every issue they cover,
Just report the news and let "We the People" determine
which way we feel it should go,
Not your way,
What I do not admire is the super preponderance of the
entertainment world's "hires" expressing their opinions,
while "We the People" have no avenue of response,
Thank you, "Mass Media,"
What I do not admire is free media time being given
to professional sports figures explaining away
their ineptitude following failure to perform,
Who cares?
I do not want to hear someone who is highly overpaid,
explaining why they should be paid,
or what they are paid,

"GOODBYE AMERICA"

What I do not admire is the "youth" of this
country's failure to recognize "value,"
The value of all those who perform intelligent feats
of excellence that truly matter to our Nation and the World,
They recognize movie stars, sports figures,
rock and rap stars but not the leaders who make a difference,
Perhaps that is because they cannot identify them,
Who are they?
Who are our leaders of today?

Goodbye America

A Clock

Whether in the dark of night,
Or in a morning's light,
I hear deep within myself, a clock,
It is crying, "tick-tock, tick-tock, tick-tock"
Then it races with super-speed,
endless determination,
"tick, tick, tick, tick,"
Steady and swift like a lighted flame
on a candle wick,
It is announcing the inevitable end of some
living things,
It states with clarity, what its movement brings,
You cannot stop a clock without ending its purpose;
its reason for beginning,
The tick, tick, tick, tick, tick, is its heartbeat;
its own way of living,
And when the plug is pulled,
the battery removed or the wind-up runs down,
All "unsuspecting," those who check its time,
will walk away with a frown,
For clocks represent life in motion;
always a lesson to learn,
Does time stop when the hands fail to move and turn?
Or, is it resting at its split second
before it moves on again?
Simply in its own way
providing a new rhythm, a new refrain,
A clock sends a message with each tick

and tock, and tick, and on and on,
A clock with its time is as sacred
as a *Tetragrammaton (Hebrew name for God),*
So do not ever laugh; do not doubt; do not mock,
And never in life, find yourself,
without the moving hands of

A Clock

Green Eyes

How beautiful they can be,
Like emeralds shining brightly for all to see,
But, when they represent envy within,
They lose their beauty and quickly dim,
For then they represent the worst
of human thought, human deed,
The seeds of want, not need,
the ultimate sin of greed,
I do not want my eyes to turn green,
If they do, the world will be able
to read my acts so mean,
How would I feel
knowing my purpose could be read?
Knowing all that could be thought about me, said,
Knowing.........by my actions,
I would become despised,
No, never let me harbor thoughts that shine through

Green Eyes

Don't Count On It

I dreamt I died and went to Heaven on high,
You know,
our "hereafter, forever home," in the sky,
I looked around for something familiar and old,
A face of a loved one, two, three...ten or more as I was told,
Nary a soul came by to say,
"Hello," or to welcome me home,
So I began to wonder,
"Where is everyone, beyond the dome?"
It seemed like an eternity, yet there was no night,
I cannot deny it, my spirit began
to gather some fear, some fright,
I was not tired, yet wondered, "Should I sleep?"
Or was I in a new world of constant deep?
I kept repeating an old familiar Psalm,
"...and I shall fear no evil, for Thou art with me,"
I cannot even peek around a corner or two;
there are none that I can see,
There are no barriers to stop me
from moving on – keep on going,
The air around is clean, it feels like a fan blowing,
Oh, my, "What is that I see ahead?"
Not one, but many gates; this was never said,
What should I do; how many choices
do I have...one, two, three...ten?
Should I push any? When?
Somebody talk to me, "gimme" a bark,
a meow, a known word or two,

"Okay the joke is over, tell me what to do"
A booming voice replied, "Choose a door,
You have made many choices before,
There is no "Map-Quest" here my friend,
You have reached the 'hereafter,'
the promised, living end,"
"But can I have a hint
about where I might belong; where I might fit?
Speak up, speak up
Will anyone answer?"

Don't Count On It

In Days Gone By?

Little girls were little ladies,
who learned to wash and sew,
They had a job in life to do;
raise the children, knead the dough,
Cook and clean and guide all the tiny tots,
Keep them busy, ever learning,
creating their Camelots,
Little girls were little ladies
in pink dirndl dresses with socks to match,
Pocket books and hats and gloves,
for little boy's eyes to catch,
Little girls who believed and dreamed on wishes
cast upon the stars in the sky,
Can those dreams and such a family life
only be found...

In Days Gone By?

Illegal

This is the word that all the "bleeding hearts" fail to recognize
when speaking about "the illegal immigrants,"
Does anyone know the definition?
Does anyone know what it means?
Why would you want to welcome to your country
a bunch of people who break the law upon stepping on its soil?
Those who are "sneaks,"
Those who steal their entry under the cover of night
or hidden from view,
Did they not "jump-the-line?"
Are they not stealing educational, health and housing services
without being legally eligible?
Whose pocket do they reach into to pay for their support?
They live a lie every day
and apparently feel none the worse for it,
And then,
when the free soil beneath their feet gathers some heat,
they march, they demand, they fly their flag above ours,
They change our National Anthem,
They change the language of our land,
If I were Hispanic, I would be embarrassed knowing
that other immigrants from all over the world, learned English,
All "illegal immigrants" are
depleting the Treasury of the United States,
Their own governments
and countries are glad to see them go,

There is no hue and cry from any South American,
Central American, Mexican, or any other invading Nation,
demanding these alien citizen's be returned,
And the one word that all those who feel these
trespasses should stay, conveniently forget, is "illegal,"
It bothers me greatly, when any man or woman,
of the "cloth" speak of how reverent and religious these people are,
Or how they have altars within their homes
and attend church regularly,
They too fail to recognize the problem,
The illegals broke the law,
They steal from hard working people in this country,
The steal from others who have waited for
years to legally gain entry to our country,
And whatever they take or steal from
U.S. citizens is totally unacceptable,
They lie,
They cannot admit, who or what they are,
These are not the traits of a "religious" person,
As I recall, Jesus said, "Thou shalt not steal,"
"Thou shalt not covet thy neighbor's goods,"
Jesus took the thief who recognized his wrong doings,
asked for forgiveness, and was in no position to
correct them, to Heaven,
He left the other thief to die on his cross,
"Illegal immigrants" have a chance to right their wrongs
by returning to their countries and entering legally,
So,
If all those immigrants who are so demanding
stole entry, or services to which they are not entitled,
step back and begin again,
If they knowingly arranged for illegal documentation
to support their presence in this country,
If they work knowing that they should not be working,

Isn't there something very wrong?
What will they lie about and steal in the future?
These immigrants who march, make demands for
what they think they are entitled to, are wrong.
They do not recognize their actions as criminal,
illegal, or unacceptable,
Their traits and characteristics are not those
upon which this country was founded and grew,
Their work ethic might be super, and from what I have seen it is,
But their moral and ethical fibers are less than what they should be,
And you wonder why you are not warmly welcomed?
That is what is wrong,
It is not your color, your language, or your background,
It is your ethics,
I am sorry the Hispanics feel that they have been singled out,
Even discriminated against,
You are not,
It is all "illegal immigrants,"
However, the major problem is you have arrived en masse,
You are demanding that we
change the language of our land to your language,
You have the audacity to fly your flag higher
than the flag of our country,
You have the audacity to fly
our flag upside down and under yours,
You have the audacity to change the words
of our National Anthem,
You have the audacity to demand
that we change
our legal documents to read in Spanish,
Who do you think you are?
This is our country,
This is America,
And, who do you think will respect you

for any of these actions even if you are given a "free ride"
by our spineless elected officials?
If you continue to behave as you are, you will always
be labeled what you are,

Illegal

Music Is Amazing

I hear the beat,
My foot is tapping,
There's no need to prompt its action,
And when the music stops, my foot rests,

Amazing!

I hear the rhythm,
My body sways,
It's fed by a tidal wave of tones,
And when the music stops, my body rests,

Amazing!

I hear the violins accompanied by harps,
How sweet; how moving – how moving,
They stir inner feelings of warmth and love,
And when the music stops,
my feelings are deeply enriched,

Amazing!

I hear the drums, the fifes, the horns;
the beat is back,
Not only for the tapping foot, the swaying body,
and feelings of warmth and love,
It is the sight of my flag,
patriotism rises from within; tears flow,

The music of our country's heart and soul,
never stops,

Amazing!

Music is special,
Music is feeling,
Music is love,
Music is life,

Music Is Amazing

Your Swirling Cyclone Of Sound

The music swirls all around,
In a loud, stirring cacophony of sound,
The drums rumble like a fierce thunderstorm,
Cotton fills the ears to block the din;
it is far from the norm,
The blood boils, it reaches a peak,
The composer made the point with sound;
stamped out the weak,
And, as quickly as the bombastic instruments
make known their point,
Along came the twinkling stars; the raindrops
gently fall upon my child's head to anoint,
Oh, the emotions found in simple tones,
Crescendos, diminuendos, pizzicatos,
the tones and overtones, the silent zones,
"Do you hear me?", cried the triangle's one note,
"I am the exclamation point;
the last sound sent afloat,"
Two or three hours of light
and heavy bars; statements all,
But a simple note on a tiny triangle
stands firm and tall,
Create away; make your inner most feelings known,
With every note, every sharp, every flat, every tone,
We will listen and critique;
love or hate the heartbeat you felt and found,
You bared your very soul, for the world to see;
your music to hear;

Your Swirling Cyclone Of Sound

Your Leaning Posts
Introspection

───────⋇───────

When you lose a loved one, you question your
ability to stand straight and tall,
How much do I really know,
and how much taught, can I recall?
Am I just a parrot of a person; what will I
miss most?
For now I realize, how much I used my parents'
strength; they were each a leaning post,
What will I do, when they are both gone?
Will I be weaker, or stronger,
or try to be what I am not; what face will I don?
You watch your guideposts, mom and dad
fade like each season's trait,
The hugs grow stronger,
but patience becomes a costly freight,
Remember the tolerance and love they gave you,
what you needed to endure?
Whatever inconvenience comes along,
return the comfort; your turn, you are now mature,
Think of how many times you simply asked
over and over and over again, "Why?"
And accepted their repetitive ways,
the merry-go-round of their minds, before they die,
You know deep within, why your pain is so great; you
recognize your own grief, the things you will miss most,
For soon, they will be gone - these lifelong friends,
your teachers, your strength,

Your Leaning Posts
Introspection

My God & I

To many, God is wrapped in ethereal bliss
far away,
But not to me; He is with me every day,
He shares my pain, my grief,
my failures, success and joy,
What I think, what I say, what I do;
what methods I employ,
He is not a stranger; He is my soul, my heart,
He sees me through, as long as I do my part,
He laughs with me when I laugh; He dries my tears,
And this has been a lifelong friendship,
through my years,
Will He be with me at my final breath;
will He hold my hand, when I die?
Guaranteed, He will be there; together we will be

My God & I

Angels Deserve The Right To Relive The Joys They Once Knew... Don't You Think?

Let's have the angels in heaven
cascade down on silken string,
To join with all of those in the world
with whom they used to sing,
Let them relive the joy they once knew
as they walked on earth,
And find all the good moments
they shared, from death to birth,
And when their spirits have been
saturated through with that joy,
Let them journey home on "ship's ahoy,"
Back to their solitude; their eternal rest,
Humming the old songs they used to sing;
the ones they loved best,
Surely, that would make me smile
and share many a wink,
Because, I believe that

Angels Deserve The Right To Relive The Joys They Once Knew... Don't You Think?

Goodbye Wisdom?

Today is the day!
My last wisdom tooth will be removed,
Does that mean some wisdom goes with it?
I still wonder why
they call all the other big "chompers," molars.
And then
reserve the word "wisdom" for the four back teeth,
They hide, you know,
Way back in the darkest recesses of the mouth,
Sometimes they hide even deeper,
They try to stay hidden,
They remain impacted,
Wisdom is like that,
It is kept for special occasions,
In fact, sometimes, it never reveals itself,
Think about it,
Our four wisdom teeth are
usually the last to arrive,
That mimics wisdom,
which grows over the course of a lifetime
Isn't that strange?
And now, today,
the final vestiges of my mouth's wisdom
will be removed forever,
Forever –
So I say, "Goodbye tooth,"

Goodbye Wisdom?

No You Don't! It's Enticing, But Not Wise

How many times in life have I wanted to
say something, but refrained?
There are some who chose, when they reached a
certain age, to say whatever they wanted to say,
I got over that in a hurry by listening
to someone much younger than I,
Debbie gave me sound advice,
"No matter how you feel,
and no matter what age you bear,
it is not a license to say what you think,"
She was far more mature,
successful and wiser than I,
I listened and learned,
You can learn from the young you know,
"Being more mature should set the tone
for much greater level-headedness,
Don't you think?"
When the "urge" to speak,
and say what you want, takes hold,
Step away from that "urge,"
Back up,
Take a deep breath,
Compose yourself,
And take pride in the fact
that you remained restrained,
Old adages are "old" for a reason,

They survive, because they are true,
In this case, the adage that comes to mind is…
"If you have nothing good to say,
say nothing at all,"
Anyone can be mean, nasty,
hurtful, demeaning and critical,
But to be able to smile and walk away
takes much greater strength of character,
Doesn't it?
So keep yourself in check,
no matter how "old" you become,
Always be true to yourself,
Be kind, considerate,
and mindful of each next thought,
And remember what is said,
can never be retracted,
The price you pay is too high when you think
that you have a right to say whatever you want,
I repeat,

No You Don't! It's Enticing, But Not Wise

'Age' Is Not A Privilege

You cannot just say what you want to say
when you want to say it,

If you do,
lonely you will be

Will You?

―――――――

"TROPHIES"

Trophies,

Can you lay them at the feet of the Lord, God,
when you enter the gates of His Kingdom?

Will His interest center on your awards,
medals, great press-releases?

Or, will the ledger record the number of hugs
and kisses shared with loved ones; those in need?

Will you be able to step forward
and gaze into His eyes and say with all honesty,
"I did my best?"

Will You?

If Only I Could

If only I could tell the young
about the future – their future,
What they should know,
What they should expect,
What changes life will present,
Some of my elders tried to tell me,
I listened,
But, rarely believed,
Now, and only now, that I am in
my "elder's age," do I understand,
The young never listen,
Why doesn't anyone listen?
Time is running out…

If Only I Could

Tomorrow

*Tomorrow: Wandering into tomorrow...into the light
of pure speculation and greatest hope. Maybe seeing
and finding some wishes coming true. Speculation
in a new, changed and different world.
Perhaps:*

**Meeting those in long residency in their new tomorrow-land
Finding answers to unsolved mysteries
*Being able to read the minds of those who ruled
before, during and after our lifetime – all world leaders
(alive and deceased), family, friends, etc.
*Unearthing the reasons for disasters (natural and manmade)
*Discovering the answers to all the WHY's (Including
why I acted the way I did every minute of my life)
*Being able to look into the future of the
world I left behind – ad infinitum
*Finding all the things I failed to mention and imagine
*Continuing to hold onto a living spirit that permits me to function
and provide an ability to think and understand all thoughts*

*Therefore, what then could be wrong with speculation –
particularly one without a need for evaluation and criticism –
simply living in a continuous state of "I want to know" mode.*

*Given this,
I'm sure a New Exciting Life waits in our tomorrow!*

That Life Span Certain

EVERLASTING?
"REJUVENATE? REINCARNATE?

Ah, you have had a face lift,
Thank God for that scientist's gift,
You have replaced a knee
and a hip; you have got more pep,
Now, do you not feel 20 years younger,
and quite hep?
But life just has so long a span,
For us to survive in the human clan,
Pessimistic? No. Optimistic? No.
Simply right on!
Time meters out our time;
then, we are gone,
That is why each moment of each day
is such a treasure,
Daily we face the unstoppable, time
and the moments we measure,
Unless of course, you believe in
mortal reincarnation,
I must ask? Will you choose your new life
and its destination?
And will your reincarnation multiply,
one for each time you die?
Reincarnations ad infinitum, my faith would deny,
I am scheduled for everlasting life – peace and rest,

A Heavenly home forever at best,
But, if I had a choice, what would I choose?
If it were something that lives forever,
serves a purpose, I shan't lose,
Once asked, I said that I wanted to be a cloud,
Float free over earth; to be quiet, and at will, loud,
In other words I defined something within
the realm of my understanding,
Something unique, different, tantalizing,
Something within the realm of my limited
knowledge and in a human term,
But my experience is an obstacle
and my ability, limited; that made me squirm,
I am not intelligent enough to know what
to choose, even if asked to be born again,
And would it be a life certain?
Eternity is an elusive thought that is trapped
in humanity's mind,
Reincarnations and rejuvenation are simply speculations –
wishes of some kind,
All I know is our Creator has a plan; we a final curtain,
And because I live, I am a part of that mystery –

That Life Span Certain

However ...

Like a child, I live to learn, and I still
have so many questions.
But, I have also lived. So, where should I begin?
With a question no doubt.

Am I A Living Dream?

Could I be but a living dream?
A result of someone else's thought beam?
Have I been created to live out
another's inner life?
A marionette dancing to
that spirit's pitch pipe?
Is my spirit mine, yours, yours?
Are we ironing out a previous soul's flaws?
Aren't we all human prototypes?
What a thought –Yipes!
Could I be a figment in
a Master Creator's scheme?
Now, I lay me down to sleep, wondering

Am I A Living Dream?

Oh, My Soul

My soul, my soul, 'Come out,
come out, wherever you are,'
A lifetime of hide and seek,
Do I ever think about my soul –
my inner character?
Not really,
Because, I feel it is quite transparent,
That is not to say, simply, a spirit, a ghost,
My soul is me,
It is who I am, what I be,
It is 'solely' and 'souly' mine in life and death,
Not a figment, not just my imagination,
And, it is the only part of me
that will survive my demise,
It is my immortal being – my immortality,
It, however, belongs to my Creator,
And that brings to light many interesting thoughts,
Can Eternal Life be considered reincarnation?
And, if a spotless soul be placed within a thief,
will that soul change its behavior?
Will the opposite occur, if the thief's soul
is placed within a good person's body?
What is a 'good person?'
Will consideration be given
to the levels of theft acts?
If I steal a pencil, is that act less wrong than
robbing a bank, or stealing someone's husband or wife?
Is theft, theft? Consider felonies and misdemeanors,

Of course, this is human societal thinking,
How might theft be judged in the courts
of the Heavenly Eternal?
Even God, through one of his Son's final acts,
forgave a thief,
Are all souls pure, when assigned – given at birth?
Oh, my soul,
Be thou worthy of Eternal Life?
How I wonder,
Will the choice be mine, Eternal Rest or Reincarnation?
Does my soul represent the genes of history?
Oh, my soul,

Oh, My Soul

Dawn

Dawn quietly slips into a new morn,
Without a sound
it sings its beautiful silent song,
And depending upon the season
it chooses it hues,
To dot the magnificent sky canvas
of beautiful blues,
No pinks carry more vivid tones
in a deep rosy, flame bright shade,
Shining no doubt, for the benefit
of clouds to roam and wade,
With the most brilliant silver and grays
that bless the cold of a bitter winter day,
When the clouds seem to move with
more speed and fury; perhaps to get away,
No matter what time of year
the sky says quite a lot,
It speaks with absolutely no 'tommyrot,'
With both boldness and peace,
it announces another day – no time to yawn,
It is a beginning,
an awakening, a new start; it is

Dawn

Tomorrow

Tomorrow?
Will it come?
Will I wake to the wonderful environs
I love so dear?
Or, will I wake to see
the faces and smiles of those who
warm eternity?
How can I judge what I do not know?
I know what I have, but what will I get?
With all its heartaches, stress and sorrow,
My life is my life; a mixture of good and bad,
sunshine and rain, heartaches and joy,

Tomorrow?
No one knows what it will bring,
Yet, we all live as though it will come,
But will it?
Do you have some guarantee
that I do not?
Why do we live the way we do?
Why do we do the things that we do?
Would we change,
if we knew it would never come?
This thing we call,

Tomorrow

"What Will Tomorrow Bring?"

Tomorrow – first, you must see another day;
welcome it with a prayer,
Be delighted to see the sun rise,
breathe the air,
It is a wonderful moment
to know that you are alive,
See the clouds frolicking in the sky,
What will I do today
to make it a day to be proud?
Quietly make someone else's day special;
this to myself I vowed,
Put a smile on someone's face,
Make the world for them a better place,
It usually does not take much,
A call, a nod, a pleasantry and such,
Make a joyful noise to the Lord;
in His name do a precious thing,
And when the day ends, smile,
be content, and wonder anew…

What Will Tomorrow Bring?

How Will I Know?

———————

How will I know when I die?
When all that is familiar disappears from my eye?
When sounds fade to no sound at all,
Will I know when I breathe my last breath and
feel my hand fall?
Will I feel my soul rise in flight?
Rise into the unknown dark of night?
Will I find the hereafter golden glow?
Feel the steps of the Heavenly ladder
situated just so?
As a spirit, should I not be able to fly?
And like a bird, climb higher than high?
What will happen to all my treasures on *Earth*?
Will they have the same value, as
I placed on their worth?
'Possessions,' 'things,' 'stuff,' junk to some,
But they do not know their history,
from whence they did come,
Who held them close, before they became mine?
How they were always warm and welcome,
like a good glass of wine,
Not to worry, they will move on to their next life;
new owners in tow,
Funny, the 'stuff' lives on, and I have to go; hmmm,

How Will I Know?

Again, The 'Stuff' Stays

I find it amusing, downright funny,
I die, and the 'stuff' lives on
to enjoy another tomorrow's sunny,
I guess
it does not have any meaning, after all,
That dresser, sofa, table against the wall,
Or, that necklace that drapes just so;
the bracelet on my wrist,
All the material items of value,
take on a strange twist,
They really do not mean a thing,
Once your soul departs and takes wing,
Isn't it funny what we consider
important in our living days,
We must go; we have no choice, but

Again, The 'Stuff' Stays

That Very Special Dawn

I looked up into the Heavens
and what did I see?
Not the sun and clouds, moon and stars, but
those who had gone on before me,
My, how crowded it is,
Spirits bumping into each other, "gee whiz,"
I imagined them to pass through each other –
a ghostly crew,
I always knew there would be a mob –
many, not few,
After all, think of everyone who has left this *Earth*,
As many as have lived life, and survived birth,
There they were pushing and shoving
like on a crowded train,
Perhaps they were the newest additions
finding space in which to remain,
I could not identify anyone by name or face,
And really, too many I have forgotten
who shared with me, this *Earth* place,
Family and friends,
associates and acquaintances, each and all,
Who were resting prone, but now standing tall,
They moved from solid to spirit,
dense to sparse – invisible,
However, *Earthly* actions seemed to prevail;
some were even incorrigible,
Perhaps they were struggling still
to learn new ways,

I wonder if they were given a time frame,
say, a few days,
Then off to darker spots; a lower level cave,
As I observed,
some souls were drifting down with a wave,
How come I was blessed to see this scene
this morn?
A preview of that special future day...

That Very Special Dawn

The Backlog

When thousands are killed in one day,
how does Heaven handle the overload?
It is easy, if we all have an assigned number
and they have a long road,
And, if the angels are computer proficient,
and they run without a glitch,
I mean the computers, not the angels; for each
new resident must have an assigned "niche,"
I do not know about confessions or life histories,
on long play in review,
They must have emergency systems; I am sure they do,
Can you hear someone calling on God, asking for help
at the check-in?
I wonder if that would be considered some form of sin,
I will give that some thought, but I do know
what I hate is waiting in line,
Particularly when I am hungry and it is time to dine,
But can you not just picture that scene?
I wonder if any thought is given to spirit hygiene,
And no doubt, there will be those
who will buck the line and jog,
'Oh, please, if I am in that mess,
let everything run smooth' to erase …

The Backlog

Heavenly Home

Is there only one gate?
If so, there must be quite a long wait,
I assume, being spirits, they should move quickly,
That could change when the gate is approached
by "catastrophic event" souls,
My, my, St. Peter would
certainly need help,
To say nothing of the angel-wing makers,
Theirs would be an exhaustingly daunting task,
Can you picture all the little cherubs
with fluttering wings awaiting their charges?
They must assure each new resident that their new
perfect wings will fit,
Then lead them to their new homes,
Their job is quite exacting
when you consider all the stars,
They have to find the right address and
turn on each twinkling light,
That is probably why the day after a storm,
or an unusual event, is clear,
Better conditions in order for the cherubs
to accomplish their work,
And the spirits would undoubtedly move swiftly,
not be water-logged and slow,
Yes, that is why clear, crisp, bright sun
follows torrential downpours and hurricanes,
Nature is proud of itself for washing the Earth;
cleaning everything in sight,

And that is the way it must be in Heaven,
Unchallenged, with expediency; efficiency to a fault,

But after the Gate is stormed,
and everyone has found his home –
all will be beautiful and serene,
I would imagine that there would have to be
a "Holding Pen" for the "Pesky and Peaky,"
Those who never found time to change their ways
or ask for forgiveness,
What will their fate be?
I can see the individual interviews now,
Every soul's language would have to be the same,
Converted upon arrival, no doubt,
There could be no misunderstandings,
And definitely no secrets,
Thoughts would be bared,
And that in itself is scary,
Not knowing what waits on the side
of the Great Divide,
Imaginations could run amok,
Not to worry, it will all be sorted out
in the Land of Perfection
As you prospect and lay claim to your new,

Heavenly Home

Laughter In The Great Beyond

Think eternal, beyond the beyond,
A New Year celebration, gathering with
those you loved and with whom you were so fond,
All those who gathered together while on *Earth*,
Pockets of family and friends,
coming together for a time of rebirth,
The liquid libation would be simple joy;
the banquet table filled with love,
After all, we cannot think in terms of life
on Earth if we are above,
And for any spirit who could not break away to make the trip,
an invitation will be sent,
Give them a day to travel from their present assignment
wherever they went,
The gatherings would be small,
so everyone would get a hug and a kiss,
And then, we could recall the best times of all;
simply reminisce,
Only reliving our moments of greatest pleasure,
Moments we hold in memory;
the special moments we still treasure,
We would all be as we were at a
particular moment and time back then,
Reliving our history; the best times –
the unforgotten,
Celebrate our birthdays,
indulging in all treats,
Celebrate holidays with appropriate

breads, meats and sweets,
We would have to stuff a year of
those special times into one day,
We would start at dawn and
end when daylight went on it way,
It would be just one of many days
with each different group,
Each starting with a giant 'war hoop,'
A time for 'can you top this' –
on the memory scale?'
This type of party really cannot fail,
And so, we would take time to stroll
down memory lane…then move on,
Capture the next cluster of known gatherings
in ethereal bounds to share…

Laughter In The Great Beyond

Listen, the Universe is speaking...

A Mystery, A Multi-Mystery

Oh, magnificent spheres of mystery,
floating giants,
Whispering descants of the universe,
earthly "observants,"
We observe – looking up, as you glide around,
You too, could be observing – looking down?
Perhaps you are looking up
from your perspective,
Being more objective than subjective,
Quietly forming opinions of us,
as we do of you,
Wouldn't that be an eye-opening gem –
'phew'?
Who is to say
you do not harbor life deep within?
Insulated from the likes of us,
who on occasion take a 'space-ial' spin,
My sides would split with laughter,
if that be the case,
So proud we are of our 'dominance' in space,
What a shock that would be,
Someday,
to have all our space probes evaporate – gee,
Sucked up by a cleansing vacuum
making a statement – 'clear out,'
You are our foes,
you have no right to be free and fly about,

Confine yourselves to discovering
your own history,
Leave ours, as it is –

A Mystery, A Multi-Mystery

Tomorrow

'My New Home'

Are you a world of lost dreams?
Has life taken away your desire to live?
It seems as though tomorrow will be filled
with the same turmoil as today,
And yet, it draws us into its time with hope,
Perhaps, we will rise to see things change and
be as they were in whatever "better time" of
yesteryear, we choose,
But is not the time in which we live the best time?
We cannot reach back to embrace what is no more,
Tomorrow is ours,
yesterday belongs to yesterday,
What was said and done
is just that, said and done,
But today, yesterday's tomorrow
is yet to be what we want it to be,
No matter what our circumstances,
the time is metered out for us to find
and live the memories of tomorrow,
The memories that we created yesterday,
The memories of today are yet to be chartered,
As we walk into today's night mystery,
and our lifetime ahead,
Today will live, as we lived it,
But not every minute will be recorded for posterity,
Only those moments we choose to etch

in our memory bank,
To be withdrawn when needed –
to enjoy again, when life and time beg a re-visitation,
Life has a peculiar side,
for as we live today,
we are thinking of tomorrow,
In fact, we concentrate on tomorrow,
And when tomorrow comes,
we will concentrate on its tomorrow,
Finding its future, its comfort, its joy,
Perhaps that's why today, the present,
loses its luster in the face of tomorrow,
And, its tomorrow…
and its tomorrow…and its tomorrow,

Tomorrow

Tomorrow is everlasting, but it holds within it,
a replicating, unending thought of the end ...

The Reason We Die

By-pass an Eternal call, 'Time to go,'
We all love life, it is what we know,
Why would we choose an unknown
mystery?
Who do you know who did that
down through history?
Most choose life, and if they could,
would choose to lose it, never,
The fear in death is in not knowing
God and the Land of Forever,
The fear of death is hinged on one's faith,
belief,
Without it, there is no crutch for relief,
Most times, we lose our will to fight
the thing we value most – life!
Everything we must do becomes a burden –
heavy drum; no more a light, uplifting fife,
We run out of energy and steam;
we need more and more help to survive,
Simple tasks become heavy duty;
yet the mind is quite alive,
It says, 'you can do it!' – Try!
But after a while,
even your body rebels – Why?
It is a strange dichotomy – it is in reverse,
The mind and the body think alike;
become perverse,
We can no longer compete with life's demands,

Its insatiable wants, and needs; its commands,
Both the body and mind, together renege;
give up their contract with life – do not ask, " why,"
If it is not the call of the Eternal,
it's definitely life losing the battle over life…and that's

The Reason We Die

I like to think of death simply as another wonder. Yes ...

Death, Just Another Wonder

Death comes unannounced;
mostly without warning,
We disappear
as the vapor finds a new dawning,
Eternity is found in what most believe,
And sometimes people even grieve,
Some insist when you draw
your final breathe everything ends,
Others cannot wait to join
family and friends,
Closing the casket lid opens a party royal,
For which they,
throughout their lifetime, did toil,
But that is not always the case, because
death, like life, is just another wonder,
The same as nature's beauty –
sunshine, moonlight, thunder,
It has held humanity in its grip
throughout history,
Why? Because it is undefined ~
life's greatest mystery,
Many have certain beliefs;
share what it is all about,
But skeptics hold true to course,
never give up their doubt,
What is this hypnotic spell we all live under?
Why don't we all accept it
for what it was meant to be ...

Death, Just Another Wonder

The Ladder Of True Liberation
"The Rising Soul"

—————

I am climbing the ladder of true liberation,
It is most peculiar,
There are no steps, or are there?
I know that I left my body,
I am a spirit,
And yet I cannot fly as spirits do,
to reach the Promised Land,
I find, I must walk,
Climbing, one indivisible step at a time,
Why can't I just rise like the mist
on a cool summer morn?
Perhaps the pace is based upon good deeds and bad,
It is unfortunate that I did not know that before,
Wouldn't that knowledge have changed my direction?
Maybe,
But now, given the length of my life,
it will take eons before I reach my destination,
The summit, of course
The top of …

The Ladder Of True Liberation
"The Rising Soul"

That's The Tomorrow We'll See

When we receive tomorrow's call,
How many will shudder and prostrate fall?
For we know not where we will be going,
What seeds we will be sowing,
Life as we know it
will change forever,
Humanity, our world and we, obviously
will no longer be together,
What lies ahead is hidden from view,
What if anything, will we be asked to do?
Rest, rest, and sleep on in an
everlasting state,
Or will we in spirit move on –
constantly migrate,
Each one's journey is his alone,
Will it be one self-sown?
Consider the Power that gave us life and birth,
Will that Power decide our worth ~
our value to another *Earth*?
Will our 'Afterlife' – the 'Hereafter'
meet our expectations?
Will it be many moments of renewal
and celebrations?
Or, will it be the end of the saga,
our book; the final stage?
Without even another entry or turned page,
The story is finished after all,
Our play has reached the final curtain call,

Time to move on to the vast unknown,
A place of peace and rest
or fantasies overblown?
I guess whatever we envision it to be,

That's The Tomorrow We'll See

Part Of My Eulogy

"THE FINAL, FINAL WORD"

"Lastly,
Do not cross my hands upon my chest,
just stick my thumb upon my nose,
So I can gaily salute all those
who did not like my prose,

That would be great,
to finally have an unanswerable word,
And know that I will travel my final
journey having been at last heard."

My Legacy

Who will remember me, when I'm gone?
What will I leave, when I pass on?
How long will the memory last?
I will venture a guess; it will pass fast,
I have no children to boast about
or say, "They're mine,"
No blood relations – no family line,
So then, what will my legacy be?
I hope my words, phrases, poems
and stories, the world will see,
There are so many to be viewed;
some even worthwhile I hope,
They embrace humor, pathos; questions on life;
some give advice – tell how to cope,
Some are downright silly; turn the world
and known concepts upside down,
Readers have said, 'You cannot say that! I smile
and frown,
That is one of the beauties of creativity and
an active imagination,
Everything you see and hear can be a contradiction,
Fantasy and reality are just a thought away,
A rainbow, or an ocean's flow into a bay,
Every face you have ever seen,
Every place you have ever been,
A snowflake with its hundreds of diamond crystal
shining bright,
Every star you can see on a clear dark night,

I want my legacy to be what I have seen
and shared in life – good and bad,
All the intricate, miniscule moments of joy;
each a touching ballad,
I do not want my legacy to be one of
a gift of silver and gold,
I want remembrances of tender memories,
laughter; let my music unfold,
Note my joy, when whistling at will,
Or, when finding a beautiful flower;
hearing a bird trill,
I want others to see what I see and feel what I feel,
Take a spin on a paddle wheel;
sense God's presence when in prayer they kneel,
I do not want my legacy to be one of property,
No, I do not want my life perceived as poverty,
I would accept being known for my diplomacy,
advocacy, literacy, and even lunacy,
For me, that is my life, and that will be...

My Legacy

The Eyes Of God

When I leave my earthly home, and
they place my remains in or on the sod,
Will I come at last face-to-face with
the eyes of God?
Or will I first take my mother's or father's
hand, as I did when I was a child?
To be led to the "Precious One" on
the other side of wild,
To journey where billions of
other souls have walked?
Will I communicate as I used to,
when I talked?
Will I be able to laugh and chatter,
or simply smile and nod
When and if, I'm in the presence of my God?
Will my parents present me in light of my life,
as the one they so thoughtfully trained?
To be held accountable as their protégé,
with their knowledge engrained?
Or, will I be judged on my own life's ledger;
my own life's deeds?
Will they be considered a beautiful bouquet
or a vase of withered weeds?
Will my deeds register as "top-of-the-line?"
Or rest in mediocrity,
less than acceptable, less than fine?
You can be sure this scenario doesn't appeal to me,
at this late date,

To be considered less than "first-class,"
only a piece of freight,
Maybe that's why older folks often are filled with
such a sense of trepidation, a sense of fear,
They realize that the scale weighs heavier on years past and
so much lighter on the remaining years so dear,
Is it too late to take inventory, to review
what I've done; would that be a crime?
Then rush about to prove my worth
within my remaining time?
Make the seconds tick slower,
I'll change; I know the road I must trod,
Before I face the judgment of my years, and look into

The Eyes Of God

This Potpourri of Poetry is
all about life, beauty, meaning, joy, sorrow,
friendships, family, special moments that run with fun.
It's about spirit and dreams.
It's a mini-memoir.
I define my life's journey and share my legacy.
And, if I have one piece of advice to give, it is this …

NEVER GIVE UP!

Build on Yesterday, Today!
Then perhaps, your Tomorrow will be what you
want it to be without even knowing
what it has to offer.
That's life!
Awaken now…
Remember, life does not provide any guarantees.

So, no matter what…

NEVER GIVE UP!

Live it – Life is magic

Author's Biography

After a lifetime of deep faith, searching for answers, and teaching, Jeanette has come to know, innate or learned, "We are our belief." As we mature, soul-stirring thoughts of tomorrow become paramount. Those thoughts, led to dedicated, prolific writing in many genres. Native Brooklynite, now residing on Long Island, NY

Printed in the United States
By Bookmasters